SAILING BY STARLIGHT

Sailing by Starlight

*In Search of Treasure Island and
Robert Louis Stevenson*

by Alex Capus

Translated by John Brownjohn

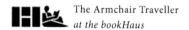

The Armchair Traveller
at the bookHaus

This edition has been translated with the financial assistance of
Pro Helvetia, the Arts Council of Switzerland

prohelvetia

First published as *Reisen im Licht der Sterne. Eine Vermutung*
by Alex Capus

First published in Great Britain in 2010 by
The Armchair Traveller at the bookHaus
70 Cadogan Place, London SW1X 9AH

This paperback edition published in 2013

A CIP catalogue record for this book is available from the British Library

ISBN 978-1-907973-74-1

Typeset in Garamond by MacGuru Ltd

Printed and bound by CPI Group (UK) Ltd, Croydon, CR0 4YY

'Well, what's he here upon this beastly island for? I said HE's not here collecting eggs. He's a palace at home, and powdered flunkies; and if he don't stay there, you bet he knows the reason why! Follow?'[1]

Captain Davis in Robert Louis Stevenson's *The Ebb-Tide*,

written in 1890 during his first year in Samoa.

Contents

Preface

MY FATHER IS A NORMAN like his father, grandfather and great-grandfather before him; all of them the sort of big, strong, phlegmatic men whose taciturnity is indicative not of any special profundity, just of taciturnity. Our family always spent the summer at a small farm in Basse Normandie which an aunt by marriage had inherited long ago. It must have been early on the morning of 6 June 1964, the 20th anniversary of D-Day, when my father dumped me on the back seat of his fire-engine red Renault Dauphine, ushered his father into the passenger seat, and drove north along winding country roads to some place on the coast – exactly where, I don't know. I have a hazy recollection of uniforms and brass bands and solemn speeches. I also recall that it was the first time I'd seen the sea, and that I didn't find it particularly impressive. What I have never forgotten is the enthusiasm with which Grandfather, Father and I shuffled along the beach, scuffing the sand with our shoes in search of evidence of the Allied invasion. We found hand-grenade rings, shell splinters, belt buckles, cartridge cases, bullets, uniform buttons, nuts and bolts, eyelets, scraps of brittle, mildewed leather, rusty bits of iron. These we stuffed into our trouser pockets, and I suspect that our cheeks were glowing – mine with innocent delight, Father's with embarrassment at our childish treasure-hunting, Grandfather's with shame at our irreverent rapacity.

After supper that night we sat round the kitchen fire with our hands buried in our trouser pockets, staring into the flames and fingering our hand grenade rings and shell splinters, which – I don't know why – we refrained from showing my mother or my grandmother. The big, cast-iron fireback leaning against the wall at the rear of the hearth gave off a pleasant warmth, and it may have been then that Grandfather mentioned that valuable hoards of gold and silver were sometimes concealed behind such slabs of metal. It struck me that there couldn't be a better hiding-place, for what thief would dare to reach through the flames and grip that hot slab of iron?

FORTY YEARS AND 37 DAYS have gone by since that night. Grandfather died nearly 20 years ago and my father is a good bit older; I myself have doubtless become more or less what my father and grandfather used to be. But what separates me from that Normandy fireplace at the time of writing is not only the passage of the years but, quite literally, the planet Earth itself. I am sitting outside the Outrigger Hotel, high above Apia, Samoa, on the far side of the world, looking northwards across the boundless expanse of the South Pacific and reflecting that not much lies between here and the North Pole, a good quarter of the Earth's circumference: any amount of water, a bit of Hawaii, the Bering Straits, and pack ice.

My wife Nadja is lying in a hammock reading, and my three sons are playing football. I myself am here to prove that Robert Louis Stevenson's 'treasure island' actually exists, albeit in a place quite different from where hordes of treasure-hunters have been seeking it for generations, and that he spent the last five years of his life in Samoa for that reason alone.

And, as the sun sinks into the sea, I experience all the emotions of that evening beside the fire 40 years ago: my boyish delight in hunting for treasure, my father's embarrassment at his own childish behaviour, and my grandfather's shame at having delved into the relics of people long dead and past defending themselves.

Apia, Samoa, *12 July 2004*

I

Peacefully at Anchor

Having got to within 190 miles of her destination on 2 December 1889, the *Equator* could make no further headway. A little merchantman of 70 tons at most, she pitched and tossed in a storm-lashed sea, sails flapping as squalls bore down on her from all directions. The rain was torrential, the temperature 40 °C, the humidity 100 per cent. This was no sort of climate for a consumptive Scot like Robert Louis Stevenson. Had he listened to his doctors, he would have been convalescing in the cold, dry mountain air of the Davos sanatorium where he had almost regained his health after spending two winters in the Swiss Alps. Instead, he was sitting cross-legged on the sodden planks below deck, chain-smoking cigarettes and writing a letter to his old friend Sidney Colvin, a Cambridge scholar and professor of fine art. He was barefoot and dressed only in a pair of black-and-white striped trousers and a sleeveless vest with a red sash wound around his waist. Tossing and turning in her sleep beside him lay his seasick wife Fanny, and beside her, youthfully at peace with the world, lay 21-year-old Lloyd Osbourne, her son from her first marriage. The ship, which reeked of fermenting coconuts, was teeming with lice and cockroaches the size of a thumb.

> We are just nearing the end of another long cruise. [...] Rain, calms, squalls, bang – there's the foretopmast gone; rain, calms, squalls, away with the staysail; more rain, more calms, more squalls; a prodigious heavy sea all the time, and the *Equator* staggering and hovering like a swallow in a storm; and the cabin nine feet square, crowded with wet human beings, and the rain avalanching on the deck, and the leaks dripping everywhere; Fanny, in the midst of fifteen males, bearing up

wonderfully. [...] If we only had twopenceworth of wind, we might be
at dinner in Apia tomorrow evening; but no such luck; here we roll,
dead before a light air – and that is no point of sailing at all for a fore
and aft schooner, the sun blazing overhead, thermometer 88˚...[1]

Louis had been roaming the South Seas for 18 months. He had
visited the Marquesas, Tahiti, Hawaii and, most recently, the Gilbert
Islands, his purpose being to write accounts of his travels for American periodicals. This he had done to everyone's dissatisfaction. The
magazine readers were disappointed that the author of *Treasure
Island* should burden them with long-winded, schoolmasterly dis-
quisitions, the publishers were disappointed with their sales, and
Louis himself found the work a tiresome chore and couldn't wait
to get it over. He was yearning to go home, first to London, then
to Edinburgh. He had absolutely no idea at this time of settling in
Samoa, nor was there any indication that only six weeks later, at the
age of 39, he would invest all his available assets in a patch of impenetrable jungle and spend the rest of his life there. On the contrary:

I am minded to stay not very long in Samoa and confine my studies
there (so far as anyone can forecast) to the history of the late war. [...] It
is still possible, though unlikely, that I may add a passing visit to Fiji or
Tonga, or even both; but I am growing impatient to see yourself, and I
do not want to be later than June of coming to England. [...] We shall
return, God willing, by Sydney, Ceylon, Suez and (I guess) Marseilles
the many-masted: copyright epithet. I shall likely pause a day or two
in Paris, but all that is too far ahead – although it now begins to look
near – so near; and I can hear the rattle of the hansom cab up Endell
Street, and see the gates swing back, and feel myself jump out upon the
Monument steps – Hosanna! – home again.[2]

The ship lay becalmed for another three days. It was not until
the morning of 7 December 1889, the Stevensons' 26th day at sea,
that she hove in sight of Upolu, Samoa's elongated principal island,
which is mountainous and clothed in dense jungle. The offshore
breeze was laden with the scent of coconut oil, woodsmoke, tropical flowers and breadfruit baked on hot basalt slabs. Skirting the
bay was a single road surfaced with crushed white coral. Beside it,
half hidden by an avenue of coconut palms, lay the 'capital', Apia: a
few dozen whitewashed clapboard houses nearly all of which were

occupied by Europeans, most of them Germans. The largest building was the headquarters of the Deutsche Handels-und Plantagen-
Gesellschaft für Südsee-Inseln zu Hamburg (German Trading and
Plantation Company for South Sea Islands, Hamburg), or Deutsche
Handelsgesellschaft, which controlled the Pacific coconut market
from its base at Apia. Adjoining it were a few buildings with corru-
gated-iron roofs, the German, British and American consulates, the
French fraternity of Roman Catholic priests, a handful of churches,
the post office, from which hung a sign reading 'Kaiserlich Deutsche
Postagentur' (Imperial German Postal Agency), and five or six shops
selling groceries and household goods. The place looked more like a
makeshift seaside resort than a town. There were half a dozen seedy
bars where you could buy gin, brandy and soda and German beer
(Flensburger and Pschorrbräu for 1 mark 50 pfennigs in German cur-
rency), also a billiard hall, a bakery, two smithies and two cotton gins.
A little way outside town was the 'Lindenau', a German beer garden
whose Pschorrbräu was agreeably chilled whenever the monthly
mailboat from San Francisco had brought some ice, and the German
skittle club's alley was situated nearby. But Apia's major attraction at
this time was the old steam merry-go-round down at the harbour, a
last relic of some touring American showmen who had scattered to
the four winds when the boss couldn't pay their wages, leaving their
equipment behind. A French bar owner had acquired the carousel
dirt cheap, and from then on it had been set going every weekend.
For 25 pfennigs the young men of the little town could treat their
girlfriends to a ride on a fierce lion or a noble charger while the organ
wheezed away ad infinitum.

WHEN THE *EQUATOR* entered the harbour, which was threaded with
coral reefs, some Samoans came out to meet her in their graceful outriggers. They sang half-melancholy, half-cheerful songs of welcome
in their melodious language, which reminded German colonists
of Italian, and thrust their paddles into the water in time to their
singing. Tall and muscular, the men were tattooed from hip to knee
with fine, latticework patterns that made them look as if they were
wearing dark shorts under their loin cloths. The women, who wore
hibiscus blossoms in their hair, were only lightly tattooed with little
stars on their shoulders, stomachs or calves. Following the outriggers came a European boat in which stood a tall, blue-eyed man in

a white linen suit and a panama hat. This was Harry J Moors,* an American who had lived in Apia for 14 years and traded in anything that could be bought or sold. He supplied the German colonists with Australian beer, the French with New Zealand lobsters, the British with French red wine, the Samoans with guns and coloured cotton cloth. He sold coconuts and pineapples all over the world and dealt in real estate, saddle horses, ship's passages and bank credits. Harry Moors maintained several branches on other islands and knew everyone in the South Pacific. He pulled strings in the sphere of colonial policy, smuggled weapons for rebels, organized wrestling matches and theatrical productions, and was destined to become Apia's first cinema owner. Being *au courant* with all the latest tropical gossip, he had naturally heard long ago that Stevenson would be coming; his old friend Joe Strong, with whom he had drunk many a night away in Hawaii, and who happened to have married the world-famous author's stepdaughter, had written to him to ask if he would look after his parents-in-law for the two weeks they meant to spend in Samoa. No one could have foreseen that those two weeks would stretch to several years.

When Harry Moors's boat came alongside the *Equator*, the Stevensons hurriedly climbed down the ladder and joined him aboard. After a cursory handshake, Louis asked if they might go ashore without waiting for their luggage; they had been at sea for nearly four weeks and couldn't wait to set foot on dry land again. Harry Moors steered the boat carefully between the wrecks of four warships that lay around the harbour basin like bizarre memorials. Thanks to colonialist obstinacy and naval incompetence, they had been wrecked one stormy night nine months earlier. It had happened like this.

The Samoan tribes had been engaged in a bloodthirsty civil war since the middle of the 19th century. The weapons they needed for this activity were gladly supplied to them by German merchants – in exchange for real estate, of which the Samoans had no conception. In March 1870, for example, the Hamburg firm of Godeffroy & Co had acquired half a square mile of land on the main island of Upolu, complete with coconut palms, breadfruit trees and a small river of excellent drinking water, for one Snider pistol and 100 rounds of

---

*H J Moors (1854–1926) came to Samoa as an employee of the Deutsche Handelsgesellschaft. His grandson Patrick Moors now runs Betty's Hotel in Apia.

ammunition – a deal rendered all the more profitable by the fact that the gun came from the firm's own arms factory in Belgium. Within a few years, by employing this and other methods of a similar nature, Godeffroy & Co had acquired over 38 square miles of land, or about one-fifth of all the cultivable land on Upolu. The main island had thus de facto become a German possession, and the budding colonial power claimed the archipelago as a 'protectorate'. This move had been opposed not only by rival Samoan chiefs but also by the other Pacific colonial powers, Great Britain and the United States. When Reich Chancellor Otto von Bismarck underlined Germany's interests by dispatching three warships to Samoa, US President Grover Cleveland had also sent a squadron. This meant that by early March 1889, nine months before the Stevensons' arrival, six warships were lying at anchor in Apia harbour: the US steam frigate *Trenton* escorted by the corvette *Vandalia* and the gunboat *Nipsic*; and, for Germany, the corvette *Olga* and the gunboats *Adler* and *Eber*.

The world held its breath in expectation of a spark that would ignite the first German-American war. A few days later, on 15 March, the British frigate *Calliope* put in an appearance on behalf of Queen Victoria. Because the harbour was already quite full, *Calliope* had to anchor outside not far from the entrance.

This humiliation would soon turn out to be a blessing, for that afternoon the screams of the seabirds died away, the sky turned green, and all the animals ashore slunk off into the bush. The captains of the seven warships watched apprehensively as the barometer, with dramatic rapidity, fell to an unprecedented 29.11 inches of mercury. They all realized that a monumental hurricane was in the offing, and that the only sensible course of action would be for their frigates, corvettes and gunboats to ride it out at sea. However, US Admiral Lewis A Kimberley could not bring himself to vacate the harbour while the Germans were there. As for the senior German naval officer, his oath to Kaiser and Fatherland precluded him from weighing anchor first. Under these circumstances a conversation clarifying the situation would have been helpful, if not vitally important, but both sides lacked the will and ability to conduct one. Kapitän Fritze was a reserved individual who spoke little English and was thus incapable of establishing contact with the US commander. Kimberley, although just as ignorant of German, construed Fritze's lack of English as a sign of arrogance. The result was that all six German and American vessels resigned themselves to remaining in harbour and awaiting the hurricane in close and perilous proximity to the coral reef.

Towards evening an eerie silence fell. The surface of the bay resembled molten lead. The natives, warned of what was to come by the millions of cockroaches and ants that had been scuttling into their huts for many hours, seeking shelter, hauled their boats ashore. Following a last minute flash of inspiration, the captain of the British frigate fled out to sea, where his ship survived the storm unscathed. During the night, however, the Germans and Americans were overwhelmed by the hurricane, which drove great masses of water into the harbour through its northern entrance, which was open to the sea. Huge breakers came crashing down on the beach, foaming waves surged inland for several hundred yards and lapped around the colonists' groaning clapboard houses. Engines running full ahead in an attempt to reduce the murderous strain on their anchor chains, the ships fought the waves throughout that pitch-black night and the day and the night that followed it. All the lights had failed long ago, all communication between the vessels had been severed. Communication on board proved just as impossible because the roar of the hurricane drowned the captains' orders, sending them into the darkness unheard. Then water penetrated the engine rooms and doused the furnaces, anchor chains snapped, ships collided with each other and the reef, propellers were bent and rudders torn off, and by the morning of the third day of the storm four ships lay wrecked on the reef and two had been driven ashore. In all, 51 American and 150 German seamen lost their lives. The two grounded vessels – the German *Olga* and the American *Nipsic* – were towed back into the water and refloated two weeks later. The other four, which remained where they were, continued to obstruct the harbour basin for decades to come.* The Germans and Americans were so appalled by this disaster that all plans for war were shelved and the Samoan Islands declared a neutral zone.

---

*The *Nipsic* remained in the service of the US Navy for another 20 years. Roofed over and permanently moored in Puget Sound Navy Yard, Washington, she functioned as a prison ship. In 1913 the navy sold her to a private contractor, who used her as a lighter. The *Olga* returned to German waters, served as a gunnery training vessel in the North and Baltic Seas, and was wrecked in 1908. The wreck of the *Adler* remains in Apia harbour to this day. Her dark skeleton still jutted into the sky as recently as 1971, but she was buried beneath sand and volcanic rock when the harbour underwent major reconstruction. She now reposes beneath the spacious car park east of the Central Bank of Samoa.

On 7 December 1889 the whole community had turned out to welcome the *Equator* and the new arrivals. Louis, Lloyd and Fanny went for their first stroll through the town, closely scrutinized by the motley human flotsam that populated the main street and its bars. Some 300 whites lived in Samoa. Several dozen of them were German company employees recognizable by their spotless white suits, clean-shaven cheeks and well-tended moustaches. In sharp contrast to them were most of the other settlers, who went around unshaven, dressed as comfortably as possible in sun-bleached pyjamas, and scraped a living as barkeepers, small-scale plantation owners or traders who bought coconuts from the natives and sold them on to the German company. Finally, like every port in the South Seas, Apia was also home to a few dozen beachcombers: sailors who had jumped ship, bankrupt traders, failed artists, escaped convicts and aristocratic black sheep stranded there from all over the world. They spent their days and nights in huts with home-made roofs of woven palm leaves, lived on the wild fruit of the jungle, and put in a few hours' work on a plantation whenever hard liquor was unobtainable by any other means.

Unobtrusively standing in the midst of all these people was a figure in a dark but not overly smart suit. This individual, of whom more will be said, was a Presbyterian missionary named William Edward Clarke. Although he kept in the background for the time being, he was destined within three weeks to become Louis's best friend on Earth. William Clarke had been instructed by the London Missionary Society to build churches and schools for the Samoans and, in addition, to attend to the spiritual welfare of the European population. He was only 35 years old, but his greying Van Dyke beard made him look much older. He had come ashore at Apia seven years earlier, together with his young wife Ellen, whom he had married at St Columb, Cornwall, three weeks before they sailed. Clarke had soon felt at home in Samoa. Not so Ellen, who suffered from the murderous tropical climate, yearned for her family and friends, and missed the civilized amenities of England. After only two years Clarke quit the service and went back to Cornwall with his wife, but it wasn't long before he had an irresistible urge to return to Samoa – quite why, we do not know. Whether he found the bleak formality of life at home repugnant or was summoned back by some idea, plan or objective, William and Ellen Clarke returned to Apia on 17 July 1887, after only a year in England.

Many years later, Clarke described his first encounter with Stevenson as follows:

> I met a little group of three European strangers, two men and a woman. The latter wore a loose native gown, a brilliant plaid shawl across her shoulders, a Gilbertese straw hat, its crown encircled with strings of shells, a necklace of scarlet berries; across her shoulder was strung a mandolin. I noticed that her hair was jet-black, her face browned and burnt by the sun. She wore large crescent gold earrings, and her bare feet were encased in white canvas shoes. The central figure of the group was a tall, gaunt man in shirt sleeves, with a brown velvet coat slung over one shoulder, a white broad-peaked yachting cap, white flannel trousers, once clean, a cigarette in his mouth, and a camera dangling on its strap in one hand. He turned to me a pair of singularly arresting and penetrating eyes as he passed. A younger man walked by his side, clad in a striped pyjama suit, the undress uniform of most European traders in those seas, a broad-brimmed, slouch straw hat, and blue sun spectacles; he carried a banjo in one hand, a concertina in the other. They had evidently just landed from the little schooner now lying placidly at anchor, and my first impression was that probably they were a party of vaudeville artists en route to Australia or the States, compelled by their poverty to take the cheap conveyance of a trading vessel, and exploring ashore while the vessel was detained in port.[3]

There was only one hotel in Apia at this period, the Tivoli, and it was not particularly clean, so Harry Moors invited the newcomers to stay with him for the time being. If his memoirs are to be believed, he took to Stevenson immediately:

> He was not a handsome man, and yet there was something irresistibly attractive about him. The genius that was in him seemed to shine out of his face. I was struck at once by his keen, inquiring eyes. Brown in color, they were strangely bright, and seemed to penetrate you like the eyes of a mesmerist ... I needed not to be told that he was in indifferent health, for it was stamped on his face. He appeared to be intensely nervous, highly strung, easily excited. When I first brought him ashore he was looking somewhat weak, but hardly had he got into the street (for Apia is practically a town with one street) when he began to walk up and down it in a most lively, not to say eccentric, manner. He could not stand still. When I took him into my house, he walked about the

room, plying me with questions, one after another, darting up and down, talking on all sorts of subjects, with no continuity whatever in his conversation. His wife was just as fidgety as himself; Lloyd Osbourne not much better. The long, lonesome trip on the schooner had quite unnerved them, and they were delighted to be on shore again.[4]

The next day Louis borrowed a horse from Moors and conscientiously set about researching his article on Samoa. He waited for a break between two cloudbursts, then galloped along the muddy main street to the east end of the bay to interview the British consul, Colonel de Coëtlogon, about Samoa's recent warlike past; galloped back to Moors' house to record their conversation in writing; climbed into the saddle once more and sped off for an interview with the Samoan chieftain Mataafa; hurried back to his desk and wrote it all up; galloped off to see Becker, the German consul; returned to his desk again; called on the US consul, Harold M Sewall. He was on the move for a whole week, galloping indefatigably back and forth, back and forth along Apia's only street: 'Day before yesterday I was arrested and fined for riding too fast in the street, which made my blood bitter as the wife of the manager of the German Firm has twice almost ridden me down, and there seems none to say her nay.'[5]

And so the days went by. Even Christmas brought no change in the situation. Louis immersed himself in the history of Samoa, but without developing any particular liking for the island. There was still no indication that two weeks later he would settle in Samoa for the rest of his life. On 29 December he wrote to a friend and former fellow student, the Edinburgh lawyer Charles Baxter:

Samoa, Apia at least, is far less beautiful than the Marquesas or Tahiti; a more gentle scene, gentler acclivities, a tamer face of nature; and this much aided for the wanderer by the great German plantations with their countless regular avenues of palm. [...] I am not especially attracted by the people; they are courteous, pretty chaste, but thieves and beggars, to the weariness of those involved. The women are attractive and dress lovely; the men purpose-like, well set up, tall, lean and dignified. [...] Tomorrow (Monday, I won't swear to my day of the month – this is the Sunday between Xmas and the New Year) I go up the coast with Mr Clarke, one of the London Society missionaries, in a boat to examine schools, see Tamasese,* etc. Lloyd comes to photograph. Pray Heaven we have good weather; this is the rainy season; we shall be gone four or five days, and if the rain keep off, I shall be glad of the change; if it rain, it will be beastly. [...] I am writing this on the back balcony at Moors'. [...] As I write the breeze is brisking up; doors are beginning to slam, and shutters; a strong draught sweeps round the balcony; it looks doubtful for tomorrow.[7]

This is intriguing. By Christmas the missionary William Clarke and Robert Louis Stevenson were on friendly enough terms to undertake a joint voyage of exploration. One would like to know more about the two men's time together, because it was then that Louis decided to settle in Samoa permanently – a curious decision, given that there had been no previous indication of it. Why should he, who had tended towards atheism in his youth, have found favour with a bearded missionary, of all people? What had prompted this excursion, what was its destination and how long did it last? What sort of discoveries did the two friends hope to make, and what did they actually find?

Unfortunately, Clarke's annual report to his London headquarters makes no reference to this trip, nor do Lloyd's photographs include any taken at this time. Our only surviving sources of information are Louis's handwritten notes, which state that the party travelled a few dozen miles eastwards along the northern coast of Upolu, inspected some schools and paid a visit to Tamasese, 'etc'.[8] They only briefly

---

*Tamasese was a very influential Samoan chief. We do not know if he actually met Robert Louis Stevenson at the end of 1889 or the beginning of 1890. It is an established fact that in 1910 Tamasese travelled to Germany aboard a German coconut freighter – for a state visit, or so he thought. On landing at Hamburg, however, he and his wife and son and two daughters, together with eight other native girls, were housed behind bars in the zoo, where they were expected to entertain the Hanseatic bourgeoisie by dancing, mock-fighting and brewing kava, their national drink. Because Tamasese found this incompatible with his rank, he ran out into the street, jumped into the nearest car, and shouted, 'Otto Riedel!' This was the name of a Hamburg merchant who had spent many years working in Samoa for the Deutsche Handelsgesellschaft. The unknown driver, who reacted with great presence of mind, found Riedel's address in the telephone directory and drove the South Seas chieftain to Adolphstrasse. Riedel saw to it that Tamasese and his clan were treated more fittingly thereafter. King Ludwig of Bavaria visited him in Munich, and in Berlin he attended a parade on the Tempelhofer Feld and was presented to Kaiser Wilhelm II.[6]

mention a second trip he undertook a little later, evidently without Clarke. All we know is that he began by travelling some 20 miles in the opposite direction, to the western tip of Upolu. It is hard to tell what his objective was. In the west the island's volcanic ranges give way to pleasant, hilly terrain on which the Deutsche Handelsgesellschaft had established many square miles of coconut plantations. There wasn't much to discover there, so it is quite possible that Stevenson left the Samoan coast behind him at the western cape and headed south to visit some secluded island or other. The fact is that, as soon as he returned from this excursion, he abruptly sank all his available funds in the purchase of a stretch of impenetrable jungle.

2

Really a Noble Place ...

L OUIS WAS BACK in Apia by 20 January at the latest. That was the day on which he wrote his Scottish personal physician, Thomas Bodley Scott, a letter quite at odds with all he had previously said about Samoa: 'I am so pleased with this climate that I have decided to settle; have even purchased a piece of land from three to four hundred acres, I know not which till the survey is completed, and shall only return next summer to wind up my affairs in England.' [1]

There, the mystery is solved, or so it seems: it was the climate. Louis was so taken with Samoa's agreeable weather that he decided to remain there for evermore. This is highly surprising in itself, because in January 1890 the rainy season in Samoa was characterized by sweltering heat and torrential downpours, as well as by frequent gales and extremely high humidity.* If Louis really did find the tropical rainy season so pleasant, he displayed a very bizarre taste shared by few other people. In his annual report for 1895, for example, the British vice-consul stated that the climate precluded Europeans from working regularly in the open air and remaining in good health. Many people claimed otherwise, he said, but anyone familiar with the country knew better. Besides, Louis readily admitted on other occasions that he was no lover of the monsoon rains. Exactly one

---

*It so happened that in January 1890, on instructions from the naval observatory at Hamburg, the very first meteorological reports were compiled by Dr Bernhard Funk, physician to the Deutsche Handelsgesellschaft, who was later to become Stevenson's personal physician and remained so until his death. Dr Funk's handwritten notes are preserved at the Ministry of Agriculture and Meteorology in Apia.

year later – the rainy season was once more at its height – he wrote to Colvin:

> My wife near crazy with earache; the rain descending in white crystal rods and playing hell's tattoo, like a *tutti* of battering rams; the wind passing high overhead with a strange dumb wuther [sic], or striking us full, so that all the huge trees in the paddock cried aloud, and wrung their hands, and brandished their vast arms. The horses stood in the shed like things stupid. The sea and the flagship lying in the bay vanished in sheer rain. All day it lasted; I locked up my papers in the iron box, in case it was a hurricane, and the house might go. We went to bed with mighty uncertain feelings; far more than on shipboard, where you have only drowning ahead – whereas here you have a smash of beams, a shower of sheet iron, and a blind race in the dark and through a whirlwind, for the shelter of an unfinished stable – and my wife with earache! [...] I have always feared the sound of wind beyond anything: in my hell it would always blow a gale.[2]

The deal was concluded at the end of January 1890. The plot of land, which Louis purchased from a blind Scottish blacksmith, was situated 3 miles south of Apia at the foot of the island's highest volcanic peak. Completely overgrown with impenetrable jungle, it cost him $4,000 – all he possessed. Not knowing how he was to raise the money to build a house on it, he estimated that he would have to dash off two or three extremely successful books in his jungle home.

> Meanwhile, I have bought 314½ acres of beautiful land in the bush behind Apia; when we get the house built, the garden laid, and cattle in the place, it will be something to fall back on; and if the island could stumble into political quiet, it is conceivable it might even bring a little income. [...] We range from 600 to 1500 feet, have five streams, waterfalls, precipices, profound ravines, rich tablelands, fifty head of cattle on the ground (if anyone could catch them), a great view of forest, sea, mountains, the warships in the haven: really a noble place.[3]

The name of the property was Vailima, which Louis – and all his biographers after him – erroneously translated as 'Five Rivers,'* and

---

*Vai = 'water' or 'river'; lima = 'five' or 'hand'. Even at the most generous estimate, however, there are only three streams on the site. The true meaning

it was blessed with wild pineapples, cacao and coconuts, pawpaw and avocados. There were also mango, breadfruit, and banana, orange, lime and lemon trees. The oranges were hard and inedible, but their juice made a mild shampoo that left the hair soft and silky. The air was perpetually filled with the stupefying scent of jasmine, night-flowering hyacinth, gardenia and carmine-red hibiscus hedges, and growing everywhere were sweet potatoes, melons and pumpkins which someone, sometime, had planted in the jungle. Louis delightedly called the place 'a magnificent forest which would be worth a great deal if it grew beside a railway terminus'.[5] He promptly engaged several dozen natives to clear the jungle. They quickly created a clearing which was never substantially enlarged in the years that followed – just as none of Stevenson's coconut, pineapple or banana plantations ever made a profit – and on it he erected a hut to serve as temporary accommodation. His letters forbore to mention that the site enjoyed an evil reputation among the Samoans, who believed it to be haunted by *aitu,* or demons of both sexes. This was because the precise spot where he proposed to build his house had long ago been occupied by a cannibal chief who had suspended a rope above his property and devoured anyone bold enough to cross it.

When a man makes strange decisions it can prove instructive to '*chercher la femme*' behind them. If any woman was responsible in this instance, however, it certainly wasn't Louis's wife. Had it been up to Fanny, the family would never have settled in Samoa and might never have sailed the South Seas at all. A gypsyishly attractive woman of 50 with dark eyes and olive skin, she liked to go around barefoot and smoked roll-ups from dawn to dusk. On the other hand, she wasn't a girl any more, but a twice-married divorcee and mother of three. She had lost her eldest child, a daughter named Belle, to

---

of Vailima, 'water in the hand', harks back to the legend of Sina, a beautiful girl who lived in the place now known by that name. She was so beautiful that Tui Fiti, the king of Fiji, heard about her. Transforming himself into an octopus, he swam over to Samoa and up the Vaisigano River, which flows into the sea in Apia Bay, and came to the spot where beautiful Sina fetched water for herself and her family every day. Tui Fiti fell madly in love with her, as she did with him. Unfortunately, however, he regained only half his human shape: he turned back into a man from his head to his hips but remained an octopus from the loins down and continued to be imprisoned in the stream. Nevertheless, Sina visited Tui Fiti every day, and in token of her love she scooped up water in her hands and gave it to him to drink.[4]

a drunken husband and her youngest, Hervey, to tuberculosis. The middle child, Lloyd, was faithfully accompanying her round the globe. Lack of talent had compelled her to abandon her youthful dreams of becoming a writer, a dancer, an artist, or at least a famous couturière. When Louis jokingly said she had 'the soul of a peasant' because of her flourishing vegetable garden she was cut to the quick and made the most terrible scenes about it for months on end.[6] 'Louis tells me that I am not an artist but a born, natural peasant,' she wrote in her diary on 5 November 1890. She hated this designation so much that she was positively pleased when the garden went wrong in some way. In recent years she had put on a little weight around the hips and her thick black hair had acquired a dusting of silver. If she had one ambition left, it certainly wasn't a patch of jungle on a South Sea island, but a well-heated English drawing-room with sophisticated guests and servants devoid of body odour. She had suffered since the beginning of their cruise from all manner of imaginary and genuine ailments. She was terrified of typhus, cholera and elephantiasis, subscribed to *The Lancet,* and felt universally threatened by vermin, parasites and poisonous insects. She was afraid of wars, natural disasters and food shortages. Where her relations with the natives were concerned, she entertained a profound mistrust of the friendliness displayed by tattooed, work-shy barbarians.

Although it had undoubtedly been a relief to her to go ashore in Apia and put a temporary end to a Pacific cruise that had covered almost 20,000 miles, during which she had been constantly seasick, this far from implied that Fanny wanted to settle in Samoa for the rest of her days. If her husband was buying up land by the square mile, it certainly wasn't at her wish, and if she'd known that he would keep leaving her alone in the jungle to go off on scouting trips, she would have managed to thwart his purchases. Things happened in Vailima that filled her with nameless dread. Even on the most peaceful days, strange, subterranean rumbling sounds could be heard in the garden. Fanny suspected the existence beneath her feet of a cavern in which lurked black men armed with knives – or, worse still, surmised that the rumbling sounds were of volcanic origin. She sometimes experienced short, sharp earth tremors; on other occasions, sulphurous fumes filled her nostrils when there was no fire burning anywhere in the vicinity.* She wrote in secret to her friend Fanny Sitwell in Scotland,

---

*That Fanny's fear of volcanoes was not entirely unfounded became clear 12 years

Because I make my sacrifice with flowers on my head and point out the fine views on the way, do not think that it is no sacrifice and only for my own pleasure. The Samoan people are picturesque, but I do not like them. My time must be so arranged as not to clash with them. I shall be able to get no servants but cannibal black boys. A great part of the housework I shall have to do myself, and most of the cooking. The land *must* produce food enough for us all, or we shall have nothing to eat. I must also manage that. Oh, it makes me tired to speak of it; and I never feel well, then. I don't want to complain. I am not complaining really, only telling you. I do want Louis, and I do want everybody to think I like going to Samoa – and in some ways I do like it; I don't want people to think I am making a sacrifice for Louis. In fact I *can't* make a sacrifice for him; the very fact that I can do the thing in a way makes a pleasure to do it, and it is no longer a sacrifice, though if I did it for another person it would be.[8]

Louis, Fanny and Lloyd led a frugal existence during their early days at Vailima. Occasional visitors reported that they had to bring their suppers with them because the Stevensons had little more to eat than an avocado pear shared between the three of them. This situation would soon undergo a fundamental change, however. In the few years the Stevensons spent in Samoa, the property attained an opulence that made even the wealthiest European merchants and the most powerful Samoan chiefs green with envy.

In the following two years there arose in the jungle above Apia a two-storeyed mansion larger and more luxuriously appointed than any that had ever before been seen in Samoa. The veranda, which was 13 feet wide and ran the full length of the house on two floors, afforded a splendid view of Apia Bay. The bathroom and kitchen were supplied with running water. The hall on the ground floor was 65 feet long and 43 wide. The parquet floor and coffered ceiling were of varnished Californian redwood (*Sequoia sempervivens*), which is much in demand in the tropics because of its resistance to mould and termites. The silverware and the mahogany and rosewood furniture were solidly English, the walls hung with family portraits, and the decor included two sculptures: a group in plaster by Rodin and a

---

later, in October 1902, when a volcano erupted on the neighbouring island of Savaii and buried most of the German plantations there beneath several feet of lava.[7]

marble bust of Louis's grandfather, Robert Stevenson, inventor of the flashing lighthouse. The big open staircase leading upstairs from the hall to the five bedrooms and the library was flanked by two Burmese Buddhas. In one corner was a big brick fireplace, probably the only one in those latitudes. No sensible person had ever taken it into his head to install such a form of heating in the tropical South Seas. A fireplace was indispensable to Louis's Scottish conception of domestic comfort, however, so Harry Moors had to import the bricks from New Zealand at a cost of more than $1,000. Sadly, the chimney never drew properly. It filled the whole place with smoke, so the master of the house gave up lighting fires after a few attempts. The bricks in the fireplace are almost free from soot to this day.

There was no road to Vailima; all the building materials had to be brought up from the harbour on horseback. Even when the house was finished, a never-ending procession of crates and barrels wound its way up to Stevenson's property. He sent for some household effects from Scotland: an oak table, some leather chairs, a Chippendale sideboard and a cupboard filled with cut glass and Chinese porcelain. On 1 July 1891 his parents' old grand piano arrived from Edinburgh at his urgent request, although no one at Vailima played. Month after month the mailboat delivered Scotch whisky and French wines by the barrel, boxes of cigars and cigarettes, big blocks of Californian ice, Parma ham, Emmental cheese and Belgian chocolate. The stables usually housed three or four milk cows and several horses, as well as pigs and chickens. Because such a sizeable establishment could not be run without help, Louis and Fanny engaged some household staff. At Christmas 1891, in addition to plantation workers, Vailima employed five Samoan domestic servants; a year later there were 12. Harry Moors estimated that the house cost some $20,000 to build, and Stevenson himself put the annual running costs at $6,500 – a very substantial sum in the 1890s.

It was a long and laborious business getting the house built. When it was finished at last, however, Stevenson seemed less enthralled by the climate or the abundant flora and fauna than by Mount Vaea, which formed part of his estate and rose to a height of 1,558 feet above sea level, its summit forever circled by wheeling frigate birds. The flanks of the mountain, which had acquired their shape from streams of congealed lava, were densely clothed in impenetrable jungle and pervaded by the cooing of the wood pigeons that inhabited its canopy of foliage. 'I think Stevenson must several times have climbed up Vaea mountain,' Harry Moors wrote later, 'for on more than one occasion he spoke to me of the "gorgeousness" of the view from the top of "his mountain".'[9]

There was no path to the summit, so Louis must have found it quite an effort to fight his way up slopes so densely swathed in vegetation. One presumes that he was accompanied by two or three Samoans who used their machetes to clear the way for him. He more than once told Lloyd, his stepson, that he wanted to be buried on the summit.

> Although it [Mount Vaea] was on our property and was always conspicuously in our view, Stevenson was the only one of us who had ever scaled its precipitous slopes. But in spite of his request I never could bring myself to cut a path to the summit. I knew it would be a terrific task, but this was not my real objection. I shrank, as may be imagined, from the association with his death that it involved. What was it but the path to his grave? And to work on it was utterly repugnant to me. Thus in spite of his vexation I always contrived to evade his desire. In the late afternoons as some of us played tennis in front of the house he would walk up and down on the veranda, and I began to notice how often he stopped to gaze up at the peak. It was specially beautiful at dusk with the evening star shining above it, and it was then he would pause the longest in an abstraction that disturbed me. I always tried to interrupt such reveries; would call to him; ask him the score; would often drop out of a game in order to join him and distract his attention.[10]

One would dearly like to know why Stevenson's attention was so riveted on this particular peak, which to the unprejudiced eye seems a perfectly ordinary hill like many others. Why Mount Vaea, out of all the mountains in Samoa, Hawaii and Tahiti? Given that he usually committed anything that exercised his mind to paper, and that he liked to see it all down in print, it is interesting that he devoted scarcely a word to Mount Vaea in his letters, novels and articles.[11] There being no written evidence on the subject, one's only recourse is to visit the scene in person.

Today, two footpaths lead up the mountain from Stevenson's house: a steep one that enables the ascent to be made in half an hour or so, and a gentler one that takes at least twice as long. At first sight, the view from the summit is what one would expect: to the north, the roofs of Apia with the harbour and an expanse of ocean beyond them; to the west, wooded slopes and jagged peaks; to the south, another range of hills; and, a few hundred yards to the east, the road which in Stevenson's time was the only beaten track to the south coast.

Further to the south-west, 166 miles away beyond the horizon, lies a small, conical island. In good weather a sailing boat or a small steamer could comfortably reach it in two days, a speedy Samoan outrigger in less than 24 hours. Seen from a distance, this island seems to be merely one of the extinct volcanoes in which the South Seas abound. Now called Tafahi and part of the Kingdom of Tonga, it rises 1,837 feet above sea level, covers 1.3 square miles, and is almost uninhabited. A few dozen Tongans grow vanilla in the north-west and go fishing for their own needs. Facing away from Samoa on the south side, however, is a secluded beach which has, since the days of Robert Louis Stevenson, been wreathed in all manner of legends.

A FEW DAYS AFTER SIGNING the contract for the purchase of Vailima, Louis gave an interview to a reporter from the *Sydney Morning Herald*:

> RLS: 'Yes, the islands are beautiful, so beautiful, in fact, that I have decided to make a home for myself there. You see, it is very difficult to purchase land in any of the South Sea Islands, but I have been fortunate enough to get a place which suits me in Samoa.'
> Reporter: 'But do you consider that the affairs of the island are sufficiently settled to justify you in settling there?'
> RLS: 'That's as may be. I shall have to take my chance.'
> Reporter: 'I suppose that you will utilize your experience in the South Seas in your next work of fiction?'
> RLS: (smiling 'humorously') 'Treasure Island is not in the Pacific. In fact, I only wish myself that I knew where it was. When I wrote the book I was careful to give no indication as to its whereabouts, for fear that there might be an undue rush towards it. However, it is generally supposed to be in the West Indies.'[12]

3

The Story of Fanny and Louis

STEVENSON'S LITERARY SUCCESS was still of recent vintage when he arrived in Samoa, and his belated recognition had come as something of a surprise. An unremarkable pupil at Edinburgh Academy and averse to becoming an engineer and lighthouse builder like his father and grandfather,* he had only reluctantly gained a law degree from Edinburgh University. As a young man from a well-to-do family, he had attracted attention mainly by sporting a flamboyant blue velvet jacket, together with shoulder-length hair and a straggly moustache. What was more, he liked to frequent Edinburgh's waterfront taverns and brothels, where he drank vast quantities of beer, smoked hashish and talked the nights away with seamen, hauliers and prostitutes. For a long time he was passionately in love with a big blonde named Kate Drummond, who divided her time between working in a factory and walking the streets. His plan to save her from the gutter by marrying her was thwarted by the fierce opposition of his sternly Calvinistic parents.

During the day Louis devoted himself to writing. It was his misfortune that nothing he wrote ever measured up to his aspirations, but that he could never rid himself of those aspirations or the urge to write. For a start, he couldn't for the life of him think of anything

---

*Robert Louis Stevenson's forebears were pioneers in the field of lighthouse construction. His grandfather Robert (1772–1850) invented the white-and-red flashing light by making two superimposed red disks rotate mechanically around the light source. His father Thomas (1818–87) introduced glass lenses that projected highly concentrated beams of light far out to sea. Of the 200-odd lighthouses now guarding Scotland's jagged coastline, 97 were built by engineers of the Stevenson family.

worth putting down on paper. He sometimes produced stilted little essays on Scotland's heroic past which were even, on occasion, printed in some academic journal or other. He wrote an operatic libretto of which nothing has survived but its unpromising title: 'The Baneful Potato'. In search of literary material he spent his summers roaming the Black Forest, cruising the Inner Hebrides, or canoeing on the rivers of Belgium and northern France. On his return he would write pretty but rather egocentric accounts of his travels. Not a line about pirates, not a word about Spanish gold doubloons, not a syllable about skeletons or remote desert islands.

There was no indication that he would ever write anything but anaemic, scholarly little essays. But then, in January 1883, his first novel was published: *Treasure Island,* a yarn for boys. It was the diametrical opposite of all he had written hitherto. No more jejune erudition, no more empty verbiage or vain introspection; just a straightforward, exciting adventure story.

What had happened?

Stevenson always insisted to the end of his days that *Treasure Island* had no basis in fact – that the novel was not only pure fiction but filched from other authors. In his fourth year in Samoa he wrote the following roguish foreword to a new edition:

> Stolen waters are proverbially sweet. I am now upon a painful chapter. No doubt the parrot once belonged to Robinson Crusoe. No doubt the skeleton is conveyed from Poe. I think little of these, they are trifles and details; no man can hope to have a monopoly of skeletons or make a corner in talking birds. The stockade, I am told, is from *Masterman Ready.* It may be, I care not a jot.[1]

Authors so seldom indulge in such candour that it makes one positively suspicious. Despite his confession, can it really be true that he stole the story? Didn't he mean to conceal the fact that the treasure island actually existed, and that he believed he knew its precise location?

To this day, biographers and students of literature continue to debate whether Stevenson based *Treasure Island* on authentic topographical features, and if so which ones. Many people plump for the Turks and Caicos Islands north of Haiti, others for the Isla de la Juventud off Cuba or the Isla de Caja de Muertos south of Puerto Rico. Others believe they recognize the coast of California in

Stevenson's descriptions of the landscape, and still others subscribe to the quaint idea that the author modelled his treasure island on the environs of his native Edinburgh. No one has ever produced firm evidence for any of these theories or even strong indications of their validity.

Just as insusceptible of proof is the most romantic legend of all: that Stevenson got the idea for his *Treasure Island* story in San Francisco harbour at the end of 1879, when he met a one-legged seaman who had just returned from an abortive search for treasure on a remote island. Alas, no biographer in a century has ever succeeded in identifying the one-legged seaman or locating the bar in which the conversation purportedly took place. But one thing will here be demonstrated for the first time: that the treasure-hunters' ship in which the one-legged man may have sailed undoubtedly existed, and that Stevenson was acquainted with its story.

It is a matter of record that he really was killing time on the San Francisco waterfront in the late autumn of 1879, while waiting for Fanny to be divorced and free to become his wife. She was still married to a charming and likeable but itchy-footed ex-soldier named Samuel Osbourne. Just 16 at the time, she had been teetering across her parents' Indiana farm on stilts when the handsome lieutenant rode by. He sported a golden Van Dyke beard and a blue tunic with brass buttons, and he was only three years older than Fanny. She was happy at first. Samuel Osbourne earned a good living as private secretary to the governor of Indiana. Fair-haired, good-looking and much given to laughter, he proved to be an attentive husband and, when their daughter Belle was born on 18 September 1858, a few months after their wedding, an affectionate father. Everything would have been perfect, had not the handsome lieutenant's sunny disposition been clouded every few months by the darkest melancholy. Always without warning and for no discernible reason, but as inevitably as the passing of the seasons, his cheerful mood gave way to despair. When that happened he tried to escape by burning all his bridges and walking out on his nearest and dearest. He gave up his private secretary's job and joined in the Civil War on the side of the northern states, tried his luck in the silver mines of Nevada and the forests of Canada, sought refuge in the arms of one of his many lady friends.

Fanny, who stayed behind each time and waited for weeks or even months, was at least reasonably well provided for by Samuel's regular maintenance payments. To pass the time she devoted herself to the arts and started to paint in oils and watercolour. She also consoled herself with one or another cultured admirer – but when Samuel Osbourne eventually reappeared at her door she always let him in. After ten years she gave birth to her first son, Lloyd, and three years later to her second, an angelic but delicate and chronically sickly boy named Hervey. In her 18th year of marriage, when Samuel still couldn't give up his lady friends, Fanny decided that she'd had enough. In 1875, however, divorce would have spelt disaster for a respectable farmer's daughter from Indiana, so the couple agreed that Fanny should undertake an educational trip to Europe and study painting there. In July 1875 she and the three children boarded a steamer bound for Antwerp, leaving Samuel behind. She had scarcely left the marital home when his current lady friend moved in – closely observed by a neighbour, Catherine McGrew, whom Fanny had instructed to transmit any relevant information to Europe as swiftly as possible.

Having landed at Antwerp, Fanny and Belle made a pilgrimage to the Royal Academy of Arts to enrol in a painting course, only to discover that women were not admitted as students. So they moved on to more liberal Paris, where mother and daughter gained admission to the Académie Julien. Eight-year-old Lloyd attended primary school, made friends with children of his own age and soon learnt French, but frail little Hervey was badly affected by the harsh autumn weather in Europe. He suffered from bouts of fever and coughing fits that kept him awake all night, and to Fanny's horror he kept asking for his father. In October the paediatrician diagnosed tuberculosis and held out little hope of his recovery. In March 1876 Fanny sent a telegram to Samuel Osbourne, who set off right away. When he landed at Liverpool three weeks later he found another telegram awaiting him: 'He is still alive. Fanny.' He got to Paris just in time to hold Hervey in his arms. The boy died at 5 a.m. on 5 April 1876. His unhappy parents buried him in the cemetery of Père Lachaise. Having little money, they were compelled to choose a grave of the cheapest category, which meant that Hervey's remains would be exhumed after five years and consigned to the Paris catacombs. Fanny and her husband spent a few weeks together in Paris, walking for hours beside the Seine and vainly striving to forgive one another. In July, Samuel returned to California.

FANNY OSBOURNE FIRST MET Robert Louis Stevenson a few weeks later at an artists' colony at Grez-sur-Loing, near Fontainebleau, where she, Belle and Lloyd were spending the summer. On sunny days Fanny would take her easel outside to paint peasants at work or a medieval arched bridge. Meanwhile, Lloyd and the village boys fished in the river and Belle, who at 17 was now nearly half as old as her mother and had inherited her Mediterranean good looks, flirted with the colony's numerous, more or less talented young artists. One July evening shortly after supper, a newcomer entered the restaurant of the Hôtel Chevillon – by way of the window, not the door. He was wearing a blue velvet jacket and had a dusty rucksack on his back, and the hotel guests gave him an enthusiastic welcome. Fanny was not unduly impressed by his dramatic entrance. In a letter to an admirer in California she described him as 'a hysterical fellow ... a tall, gaunt Scotchman with a face like Raphael [who] between over-education and dissipation has ruined his health, and is dying of consumption ... Louis is the heir to an immense fortune which he will never live to inherit. His father and mother, cousins, are both [sic] threatened with insanity, and I am quite sure the son is.' [2] Elsewhere Fanny described him as 'the wittiest man I ever met. Only I do wish he wouldn't burst into tears in such an unexpected way; it is so embarrassing. One doesn't know what to do, whether to offer him a pocket hankerchief [sic], or look out of the window. As my hankerchief [sic] generally has charcoal upon it, I choose the latter alternative.' She was equally disconcerted by his hysterical paroxysms of laughter, which he could stifle only by bending his fingers back until they hurt.

Louis, too, did not fall in love with Fanny at first sight. To begin with it was her daughter he had an eye for; she was only eight years younger than him and her mother ten years older. But Belle, too, evinced no sexual interest in him. 'He is such a nice-looking ugly man and I would rather listen to him talk than read the most interesting book I ever saw.' [3]

We do not know how long it was before Fanny and Louis became lovers. What is certain is that in 1876, 1877 and 1878 he spent the winter months in London or at his parents' home in Edinburgh and the summer and autumn with Fanny in Paris or at the artists' colony in Grez. He was confined to bed on several occasions, once with high fever and another time with an infection of the retina that threatened to rob him of his sight. Fanny was always there to put him up at her apartment and nurse him with maternal solicitude, heedless of her reputation as a married woman. But when his gratitude became transmuted into sexual passion she registered his youthful courtship with some amusement, and when he urged her to get a divorce so that she could accompany him to the altar she firmly declined. For all her love of *la vie bohème,* Fanny was loath to entrust her fate to an eccentric young man with uncertain career prospects and limited life expectancy. She did, however, allow Louis to persuade her to accompany him to London and make the acquaintance of his friends.

Sidney Colvin recalled later:

> [Fanny's] personality was almost as vivid as Stevenson's. She was small, dark-complexioned, eager, devoted; of squarish build – supple and elastic; her hands and feet were small and beautifully modelled, though busy; her head had a crop of close-waving thick black hair. She had a build and character that somehow suggested Napoleon, with a firm setting of jaw and beautifully precise and delicate modelling of the nose and lips; her eyes were full of sex and mystery as they changed from fire or fun to gloom or tenderness.[4]

What made an especially lasting impression was Fanny's habit of rolling and smoking cigarettes from dawn to dusk and her readiness to instruct London socialites, male and female, in this feat of dexterity. Louis happily pictured their future together in the rosiest of hues.

But then, on the other side of the Atlantic, Samuel Osbourne lost patience. He summoned his wife and children home, reinforcing this demand by stopping his monthly remittances. Fanny came to a swift decision: on 15 August 1878, after three years in Europe and shortly before the Atlantic was beset by autumn gales, she returned to California and her husband via Queenstown and New York.

Louis, left behind in London, was utterly desolated. His friends found it surprising that he could be plunged into such a slough of despond by a slightly greying, short-legged woman burdened with a husband and children on the other side of the world. Many of them surmised that he was tormented less by erotic passion than by the sense of honour proper to a Victorian gentleman who was duty bound to remain true to a lady whose reputation he had sullied. Louis felt sorely misunderstood. Unable to hope for any consolation from his friends and family, he decided to head for the south of France and roam the wild valleys of the Cévennes on his own.[5]

He devoted a whole month to making conscientious preparations for the expedition. These included the ordering of a sleeping bag to his own design. Measuring 6 feet by 6 feet, with an outer skin of green, waterproof canvas, it was lined with sheepskin dyed blue and incorporated a voluminous hood that could be converted into a miniature tent in rainy weather. It could also, Louis informed posterity, accommodate two persons. However, the sleeping bag was so heavy that the young writer could not carry it far, so he invested 60 francs and a glass of cognac in a good-natured little donkey, 'mouse grey and little bigger than a dog', christened her Modestine, strapped the sleeping bag to her back, and set off into the Cévennes. By day he was visited by profound thoughts and emotions which he entrusted to his diary at night – always with a view to their literary use. He used to lie there, idly smoking and gazing up at the sky. 'And yet even while I was exulting in my solitude I became aware of a strange lack. I wished a companion to lie near me in the starlight, silent and not moving, but ever within touch. For there is a fellowship more quiet even than solitude, and which, rightly understood, is solitude made perfect. And to live out of doors with the woman a man loves is of all lives the most complete and free.'[6]

Yet, although saddened by the fact that his two-person sleeping bag remained half-empty, he never dropped his beloved a line. 'To F I never write letters. All that people want by letters has been done by us. We are acquainted – why go on with more introductions? I cannot change so much, but she would still have the clue and recognize every thought.' After a 12-day ramble covering 120 miles, his diary was full and Modestine was worn out. He sold her at a small profit and returned to London. In the ensuing months he applied to *The Times* for a reporter's job and was rejected. He tried his hand as a dramatist but produced nothing usable. He wrote an essay 'On Marriage', but lack of personal experience rendered it very academic. Then, early in August 1879, exactly a year after Fanny's departure, he received a telegram. Fanny was once more living under the same roof as Samuel Osbourne in Monterey, the former capital of Spanish California, and she was ill and unhappy.

Louis, who construed this news – rightly or wrongly, no one will ever know – as a cry for help, left at once. Being unable to approach his parents for money because they strongly condemned his adulterous liaison, he booked a second-class, 'tweendecks cabin aboard a cheap emigrants' ship. The SS *Devonia* took ten stormy days to make the Glasgow–New York crossing. Most of her passengers were Scots,

Irish and Scandinavians. Through the thin cabin walls Louis could hear the clatter of their tin plates, the wailing of their frightened children and the slaps they received from their seasick parents.

> As I walked the deck and looked round upon my fellow passengers, thus curiously assorted from all northern Europe, I began for the first time to understand the nature of emigration. [...] The abstract idea, conceived at home, is hopeful and adventurous. A young man, you fancy, scorning restraints and helpers, issues forth into life, that great battle, to fight for his own hand. The most pleasant stories of ambition, of difficulties overcome, and of ultimate success, are but as episodes to this great epic of self-help. [...] The more I saw of my fellow passengers, the less I was tempted to the lyric note. Comparatively few of the men were below thirty; many were married, and encumbered with families; not a few were already up in years; and this itself was out of tune with my imaginations, for the ideal emigrant should certainly be young. [...] Now those around me were for the most part quiet, orderly, obedient citizens, family men broken by adversity, elderly youths who had failed to place themselves in life, and people who had seen better days. [...] In a word, I was not taking part in an impetuous and conquering sally, such as swept over Mexico or Siberia, but found myself, like Marmion, 'in the lost battle, borne down by the flying'. Labouring mankind had in the last years, and throughout Great Britain, sustained a prolonged and crushing series of defeats. I had heard vaguely of [...] homeless men loitering at the street corners of Glasgow with their chests beside them; of closed factories, useless strikes, and starving girls. But I have never taken them home to me or represented these distresses livingly in my imagination. [...] We were a company of the rejected; the drunken, the incompetent, the weak, the prodigal; all who had been unable to prevail against circumstances in the one land, were now fleeing pitifully to another; and though one or two might succeed, all had already failed. We were a shipful of failures, the broken men of England.[8]

During the crossing Louis subsisted on soup, bread and porridge supplemented by biscuits and whisky. He was more dead than alive by the time the *Devonia* docked at New York, but the 11-day train journey to California in an immigrants' train proved far more of an ordeal. The incessantly rattling carriages were black holes on wheels: overcrowded, ill lit, and even less efficiently heated. The seats consisted of bare wood and the beds for the night were planks laid across the seats plus pillows filled with straw. These had to be purchased from the railroad company in addition to tickets.

Dear Colvin,

I am in the cars between Pittsburgh and Chicago, just now bowling through Ohio. I am taking charge of a kid whose mother is asleep with one eye, while I write you this with the other. I reached N.Y. Sunday night; and by five o'clock Monday was under way for the west. It is now about ten on Wednesday morning, so I have already been already [sic] about forty hours in the cars. It is impossible to lie down in them, which must end by being very wearying. [...] I had no idea how easy it was to commit suicide. There seems nothing left of me. I died a while ago; I do not know who it is that is travelling. [...] No man is any use until he has dared everything; I feel just now as if I had, and so might become a man.[9]

The Central Pacific Railway train crossed the Mississippi and the Missouri and the prairies of Nebraska and Wyoming. It passed herds of cattle, fields of wild sunflowers and lonely, timber-built farmhouses, clapboard churches lost in the endless plain, windmills creaking softly as they pumped water to the surface. When the train made an intermediate stop to enable exhausted immigrants to alight in their new homeland, the monotonous song of a million crickets could be heard. If the sun was not too hot and it wasn't raining, Louis escaped from the carriage to the platform, where the air was fresher. Sometimes he climbed on the roof to write a letter in peace and quiet. 'I can see the track straight before and straight behind me to either horizon. Peace of mind I enjoy with extreme serenity; I am doing right; I know no one will think so; and don't care. My body, however, is all to whistles.'[10]

The train traversed interminable plains whose barren beauty was lost on Louis. It crossed the Rocky Mountains, whose eternal greyish-brown and greyish-black he found 'very depressing'; but then it left the last canyon behind and made its way over Emigrant Pass to the Sacramento River, passing woods and apple orchards, vineyards and wheat fields, waterfalls and lakes and dilapidated goldminers' towns, and early on the morning of 30 August 1879 it pulled into San Francisco, gateway to the Pacific Ocean.

Sadly, Fanny was far from overjoyed when her 'literary friend from

Scotland' made an unheralded appearance at her door in Monterey, coughing and wheezing and even thinner than ever before. The shabby blue velvet jacket hung loosely from his bony frame, the conformation of his rotten teeth was visible through his sunken cheeks, and his entire worldly possessions consisted of a battered suitcase containing little more than a history of the United States in six leather-bound volumes.[11] His exuberant high spirits had given way to dogged lassitude, his wit and loquacity were things of the past. Although Fanny was very touched that he had travelled half the globe and completely ruined his health for her sake, she couldn't decide whether this was reason enough for her to leave Samuel Osbourne – who had once more deserted her in favour of a lady friend. There was certainly no question of her giving the young man houseroom under the eyes of all her neighbours.

His hopes dashed yet again, Louis rented a room in the vicinity and waited. He couldn't appear at weekends because that was when Samuel Osbourne came visiting to play with the children and attempt to straighten out his tangled marital relationship with Fanny. Lloyd and Belle would never forget those awful weekends for as long as they lived: the tense silence at mealtimes, the murmur of voices behind closed doors, their father's muffled, menacing growls, their mother's despairing cries of 'Oh Sam, forgive me!'[12]

If he insisted on the rules of conduct prescribed by puritanical Anglo-Saxon morality, Sam did indeed have much to forgive Fanny, but she had as much or more. Months of indecision went by, during which she weighed up the pros and cons: her marital misdemeanours against Sam's; her husband's masculine charms against the youthful devotion of her lover; the social reputation of a married woman against the ostracism of a divorcee; and, last but not least, the financial security of a Californian court clerk against the uncertain prospects of a budding foreign author who had fallen out with his well-heeled family. She strove to convince the neighbours that her literary friend had come to the United States from England for a lecture tour, not on her account.

Meanwhile, Louis continued to languish nearby, powerless to do anything but await Fanny's ultimate decision. To make matters worse, he suffered from bouts of fever, toothache, indigestion, insomnia and terrible fits of coughing. Because all his thoughts were centred on Fanny, he couldn't get a sensible word down on paper. 'My news is nil,' he wrote to his friend Charles Baxter. 'I know nothing, I go out camping, that is all I know. [...] I shall send you a letter from there [San Francisco] with more guts than this and now say goodbye to you, having had the itch and a broken heart.' [13] He hired a horse and a light cart and drove to the Santa Lucia Mountains, intending to camp in the wilds. On the very first or second day he was taken violently ill and might well have died, all on his own, had he not been taken in and nursed by two ranchers who ran an angora goat farm in the vicinity. 'One is an old bear hunter, seventy-two years old, and a captain from the Mexican war; the other a pilgrim and one who was out with the bear flag and under Frémont when California was taken by the States. They are both true frontiersmen, and most kind and pleasant. Cap' Smith, the bear hunter, is my physician and I obey him like an oracle.' [14]

By the time Louis said goodbye to the ranchers and returned to Monterey in somewhat better health, Fanny had made her decision: she would divorce Sam and marry him. First, however, she would move to San Francisco to initiate divorce proceedings.* Louis was left alone once more. If she didn't want to compromise her status in the divorce suit, Fanny could not afford to have any contact with her lover, let alone live under the same roof with him. So Louis spent several solitary weeks while waiting for the divorce to come through, which it did early in 1880. He went for walks beside the Pacific. He collected seashells and whalebones. He started a forest fire by striking a match to test the combustibility of Spanish moss, long strands of which were hanging down from an old fir tree. The whole tree instantly went up in flames, and he narrowly escaped being lynched by some firemen who were fighting another forest fire nearby. 'I have run repeatedly, but never as I ran that day. At night I went out of town, and there was my own particular fire, quite distinct from the other, and burning I thought with even greater vigour.' [15]

Louis took the train from Monterey to San Francisco and rented a furnished room at 608 Bush Street. He had almost no money left

---

*Fanny's daughter Belle did not accompany her to San Francisco. She had recently run off with a young artist named Joe Strong and married him. It soon turned out that her husband shared her father's weakness for the opposite sex, and that he was a heavy drinker into the bargain. Belle moved in with Fanny and Louis in Samoa and remained with them until Louis's death. Joe Strong also spent several months in Samoa under the Stevensons' roof – and at their expense. Because he couldn't keep his hands off the Samoan girls, Belle divorced him in 1892, after 12 years of marriage.

and little prospect of earning any. Having already gone the rounds of all the daily papers, at first in search of a permanent post, then of occasional commissions, he eventually offered some of his prose for sale. The answer was no in every case. The Californian newspapers of those days had no demand for travel pieces and literary miniatures. Editors and readers were far more interested in nihilist bombers in Russia and socialist attempts on Kaiser Wilhelm's life, communist plots in France and hunger riots in Ireland, the emancipation of the Jews in Europe and the Boer rebellion in South Africa. What with mass unemployment and starvation, the crime wave and the threat of pogroms against Chinese immigrants, there was no room, even in the local sections, for lyrical literary musings. Louis would have had to write about the financing of tramways and teachers' salaries, about the juvenile forced labour scheme,* about campaigns for the preservation of Californian redwoods, about the pros and cons of prison reform, or at least about the seaport's incidence of murder and mayhem. However, he had yet to grasp that such subjects could provide him with a literary theme.

Because the days were long and his health currently permitted it, he went on long walks through the city with his notebook always to hand:

> The streets lie straight up and down the hills, and straight across at right angles, these in the sun, those in shadow, a trenchant pattern of gloom and glare; and what with the crisp illumination, the sea-air singing in your ears, the chill and glitter, the changing aspects both of things and people, the fresh sight at every corner of your walk – sights of the bay, of [Mount] Tamalpais, of steep descending streets, of the outspread city – whiffs of alien speech, sailors singing on shipboards, Chinese coolies toiling on the shore, crowds brawling all day in the street before the Stock Exchange – one brief impression follows upon another ...[16]

Louis made his way across venerable old Mexican Plaza and into

---

*According to press reports, the streets of San Francisco were inhabited by 5,000 10- to 12-year-old children who had left primary school with no jobs in prospect and, having nothing to do, were falling prey to vices of all kinds. A committee armed with $25,000 starting capital endeavoured to launch a 'Boys' and Girls' Cigar Manufacturing Company', which would have put the children to work and met the city's total demand for cigars. This scheme proved to be politically impracticable.

Chinatown, where he marvelled at the indecipherable inscriptions on the walls and the food shops' displays of dried fish, bizarre nuts and exotic fruit. Right next door to Chinatown was Little Italy, where there were 'small eating-shops, transported bodily from Genoa or Naples, with their macaroni, and chianti flasks, and portraits of Garibaldi, and coloured political caricatures.' Louis walked up Nob Hill, 'the millionaires' slum', home of railroad tycoons and gold-rush profiteers, then down into Little Mexico and along the waterfront to the most notorious of all city districts, the old Barbary Coast. The men there not only wore and carried guns quite openly but used them as well, and heavily made-up women leant against the walls in the glow of street lights. This was where seamen came to squander their pay while on shore leave. If they weren't careful, traffickers knocked them out in the middle of the street and bore them off to supplement the crew of some ship on the point of sailing. This was a milieu familiar to Louis from his days in Edinburgh. He haunted Mexican gambling joints and Chinese opium dens like a regular customer, joined German secret societies and frequented seamen's lodging houses, bars and dives of all kinds. 'I have been quietly eating a dish of oysters in a restaurant, where, not more than ten minutes after I had left, shots were exchanged and took effect; and one night, about ten o'clock, I saw a man standing watchfully at a street corner with a long Smith-and-Wesson glittering in his hand behind his back. Somebody had done something he should not, and was being looked for with a vengeance.'

At the far end of this rough district lay North Beach, home to the fresh scent of the open sea and the swaying masts of ships riding at anchor: huge European clippers that had rounded Cape Horn, small merchantmen from China, the East Indies or Australia, and, above all, graceful, low-lying South Seas schooners whose swarthy, dark-eyed seamen conversed in soft, melodious, sing-song voices and cast friendly glances at the gaunt, pallid fellows who walked past on the quayside.

Then there were the waterfront taverns. According to the oft-repeated legend cited earlier, Robert Louis Stevenson got into conversation with an old, one-eyed sea dog named Peg Leg Benton in an establishment known as Harry White's Bar. Benton is said to have told the young author about one of the most famous of all treasure islands, on which generations of pirates are reputed to have buried their treasure. This is Cocos Island, which lies 2,486 miles south-east of San Francisco in the Pacific Ocean, not far from Costa Rica. That the man or the bar ever existed is doubtful; but what is quite certain – and all Stevenson's biographers have overlooked this – is that in October 1879, while he was waiting for Fanny's divorce to come through, a shipload of treasure-hunters actually returned to California. The vessel attracted attention in the press. It is not, there-fore, too far-fetched to assume that Louis read the *San Francisco Call* for Friday, 31 October 1879, or a few days after he returned from the wilds. It splashed the following front-page report:

COCOS ISLAND GOLD

TWO EXPEDITIONS THAT SEARCHED AND CAME TO GRIEF

Cocos Island, situated off the coast of Central America, is popularly supposed to be thickly planted with bags of treasure, left there by the ancient buccaneers and freebooters who plundered the seas in days gone by. One tradition says that on several occasions the genial old pirates, who made the island their headquarters, sank their galleons along the shores to save their treasure, and that much money formerly belonging to Spanish merchantmen is now lying around in the vicinity. Several expeditions have gone to Cocos Island in search of these mythical millions, but none has as yet found them. The schooner *Vanderbilt*, which sailed from this port on the 12th of April last for the purpose of discovering and bringing back some of the treasure planted by the exterminated pirates, has been heard from, having arrived at Santa Barbara a week ago with a discouraged, goldless crew. [...] For three months they toiled under the tropic sun, running tunnels and drifts, and sinking pits and ditches; but their labor was in vain, and as their supplies ran low, they were compelled to leave.

Calms and light winds retarded their progress, and everything on board in the shape of provisions was consumed except flour and tea, on which the company subsisted for the last 12 days. The voyage to Santa Barbara occupied 66 days. During the trip a storm was encoun-tered, which blew away both the schooner's topmasts and came near disabling her. While the *Vanderbilt* was at Cocos Island, the steamer *Rescue* of San Francisco arrived, also in search of the fabled gold, but her Captain and crew soon became disheartened and sailed for Punta Arenas, where the schooner was sold to the Costa Rican government.[17]

4

Cocos Island

COCOS ISLAND is hard to find – so hard that generations of sea-farers claimed it didn't exist at all. Surrounded by strong and treacherous oceanic currents, overhung all year round by dark clouds and swathed in dense, hot, steamy mist, it covers just 9.2 of the 64 million square miles that make up the indigo-blue immensity of the Pacific Ocean. For ten months of the year the rain is heavy, incessant and accompanied by thunder and lightning; the rest of time it rains several times a day.

The island owes its name to the many coconut palms whose slender trunks stand out white against the green of its jungle-fringed shores. Since its discovery in 1535 by Spanish explorers, Cocos Island has been visited by countless buccaneers, whalers and circumnaviga-tors of the globe who landed there to stock up with drinking water and coconuts. Many of them cruised nearby for weeks without spot-ting the island in the mist, even though it is a typical volcanic cone 2,080 feet high. And when the helmsmen finally – and belatedly – sighted land, their vessels were often dashed to pieces against the vertical, surf-eroded basalt cliffs, which rise in places to a height of nearly 330 feet. It is impossible to land in the east, south and west. The island is accessible only from the north by way of the pebble beaches in Wafer Bay and Chatham Bay.

No one has ever wanted to live there – with the exception of the German adventurer August Gissler and his wife Clara (of whom more later), who stuck it out for 17 years in their log cabin in Wafer Bay. The steep slopes below the mountain peaks are completely clothed in tropical rainforest. Daylight never really penetrates the overhanging foliage of the giant trees, whose trunks and branches are densely festooned with sodden moss, and bromeliads grow amid their aerial roots. Visibility is wholly obscured by climbing plants and lianas, and the ground is covered with impenetrable undergrowth, elephant grass the height of a man, giant ferns, tough creepers and poisonous thorn bushes. Rain is forever falling from the dark clouds on to the treetops, from the treetops on to the ferns, and from the ferns on to the moss and lichen, whence it runs across the yellow clay at ground level to form raging mountain torrents that cascade over the cliffs into the ocean.

The island lies on a minor tectonic plate situated between the big North American and the still bigger Pacific plate. Since the plates move laterally and overlap, earthquakes and volcanic eruptions frequently occur on the fault lines. We do not know how many hundreds of thousands of years ago Cocos Island arose from the volcanic substratum, spewing fire and ash, or when the first seeds were wind-borne from the American mainland and took root in the fertile volcanic soil. At all events, it was not long before the island became clothed in dense jungle and stray birds settled there: red- and yellow-footed boobies, white terns, frigate birds, seagulls, a variety of cuckoo, the olive-green flycatcher, and humming-birds of all shapes and colours. Insects arrived at the same time: moths the size of a man's palm, butterflies, big winged grasshoppers, cicadas, wasps, cockroaches, dragonflies, mosquitoes and ants – red ants. Hundreds and thousands of the latter crawl over every stone, every tree, every bush – and any human being who ventures into the forest. Their instinct tells them to bite whenever their antennae touch something warm and alive, and the effect of their bite is intensified by the formic acid in their saliva, which causes hours-long irritation. Innocuous in comparison are the pale-green, blue and orange anole lizards, large numbers of which clamber around in the treetops. It is probable that these are all descended from a single pregnant female perched on a rotten branch somewhere on the coast of Central America unimaginably long ago, and that the branch broke off, fell into the sea and drifted westwards until it lodged in the rocks of Cocos Island. There are no snakes on the island, perhaps because they possess no limbs with which to cling to rotten branches. One also looks in vain for mammals that may have made the crossing, because warm-blooded creatures are far more vulnerable to wet, cold and hunger than amphibians and reptiles. Although there are millions of huge rats – rats on the beaches, in the ground, in the water, even in the trees – these arrived only three or four hundred years ago, when some sea captain fumigated his ship's hull while the crew were ashore. Because the ground is always sopping wet, the rats build their nests in the treetops. The females, which are continually pregnant, give birth to as many as 18 young after a gestation period of only three weeks. Thanks to their excellent supplies of food and absence of natural enemies, the young become sexually mature within a month.

Cocos Island also became home to the European domestic pig. This happened early on the morning of 30 July 1793, the day on which the *Rattler*, which was reconnoitring hunting grounds in the Pacific for the British whaling fleet, weighed anchor off Chatham Bay. Her captain, James Colnett was relieved to depart:

> We were much wearied, during the four days we passed off this island, and prepared to quit it. We therefore took on board two thousand cocoa nuts; and, in return, left on shore, in the North bay, a boar, and sow, with a male and female goat. In the other bay we sowed garden seeds of every kind for the benefit and comfort of those who might come after us. I also left a bottle tied to a tree, containing a letter.[1]

The two goats died of overindulgence on the island's abundant fauna and flora and the message in a bottle was removed a year later by Captain George Vancouver, who dropped anchor in the bay. However, the boar and the sow took to the forest and multiplied. Their descendants soon ran wild, becoming lithe, intelligent little herd animals with vicious red eyes. They attack from behind and are hard to hunt, but their meat is lean and tasty.

Finally, just to fill the cup of food-seeking seafarers full to overflowing, the coastal waters are swarming with manta rays, tuna, swordfish, sharks, bonitos, mackerel, maigres, marlin and turtles, together with shrimps, crabs, oysters and other crustaceans and shellfish without number. Although a similar abundance can be found on and around many of the Pacific Ocean's 20,000 islands, what distinguishes Cocos Island from all the others as a treasure island is its geographical position (5° 32' 57s north and 87° 2' 10s west). Located 310 miles south of Costa Rica and 497 miles west of Panama, it is out of sight of the American mainland, far from the major shipping routes and hard to find, but easily attainable, given a favourable wind, in two or three days: in other words, an ideal base for British and French pirates who had designs on the untold riches of Spanish America.

The English buccaneer Edward Davis turned up there in the *Bachelor's Delight* as early as 1684. Legend has it that Cocos Island was his headquarters, and that he raided the coast of New Spain from there for 20 years, ranging northwards as far as Baja California and southwards to Guayaquil. He was sometimes joined by other pirate ships, the *Cygnet* under Captain Swan or Captain Eaton's *Nicholas,* and occasionally by some French ship or other.

Benito Bonito, the legendary 'Bonito of the Bloody Sword', one of the most celebrated Caribbean pirate captains, is said to have buried his treasure here in 1820. He had embarked on his career in 1814 as the captain of a small Spanish privateer. Having captured a Portuguese merchantman, he used it to seize the British slaver *Lightning,* which he promptly rechristened *Relampago,* the Spanish translation of her original name. He sowed death and destruction in the Caribbean for years until the British Admiralty sent two frigates and a corvette against him. Benito Bonito escaped them by sailing the *Relampago* around Cape Horn to the Pacific side of South America. In 1819 he learned that the Spanish authorities were sending a huge consignment of gold from Mexico City to the coast on muleback, intending to ship it from Acapulco harbour to Madrid via Manila. Having landed in a deserted bay, Bonito and his men lay in wait for the mule train, massacred its military escort, and – according to legend – bore the gold off to Cocos Island.

There can be no doubt that this small desert island off Costa Rica is the mother of all treasure islands. No area in the world is reputed to harbour as much buried treasure as those few hundred yards of coastline between Chatham Bay and Wafer Bay. The countless treasure-hunters' maps in circulation for the past two centuries have been bought for good money, copied and sold on in seedy waterfront bars, shady antique shops and squalid seamen's lodging houses. If they were all genuine, anyone who drove a spade into the ground would hit pay dirt. But the most valuable and eagerly sought after of all pirate treasures, which everyone has assumed to be buried on Cocos Island ever since its disappearance, has always been the treasure from Lima Cathedral. All trace of it has been lost for nearly 200 years.

AT THE BEGINNING of the 19th century, rebellions by the oppressed peoples of America were spreading like wildfire. The 13 British colonies of North America had already thrown off the Old World's yoke.

The struggle for independence was raging in Mexico, and in South America revolutionary armies were winning victories in quick succession. Abandoning one province after another, the Spanish grandees withdrew to Lima, Spanish America's capital of capitals and then one of the wealthiest cities in the world. This was where gold from the mines of Peru was dispatched to Spain, likewise silver from the mines of Mexico and most of the treasures that had been stolen from the Incas, Mayas and Aztecs during the previous three centuries. In August 1821, however, panic reigned in Lima. Simón Bolívar's ragged but victorious troops were rapidly advancing from the north and General José de San Martín was crossing the Andes from the east. Meanwhile, the Chilean fleet commanded by the eccentric Scot Lord Cochrane, Earl of Dundonald and a former admiral in the Royal Navy, was preparing to blockade Peru from the west by sea. It seemed to be only a matter of days and hours before the venerable Plaza de Armas would be overrun by hordes of unwashed mestizos and runaway negro slaves. Although Lima was guarded by 10,000 Spanish soldiers loyal to the Crown, they were too soft and unreliable to hold out for long. It being impossible to evacuate the city, the bishop, viceroy and governor came to an agreement: the cathedral's hoard of sacred and profane treasures, which had been laboriously amassed over a period of three centuries, must at least be taken to a place of safety. And so, under the gaze of the city's marvelling inhabitants, the ecclesiastical treasures of Lima were removed from the cathedral catacombs on muleback and loaded on to ox carts: massive cedarwood chests, jewel-encrusted caskets, statues of the Madonna, crucifixes, and countless bones of saints and splinters from Christ's cross. Many of the chests were said to be brimming with pearls, opals, garnets, diamonds, amethysts, blood-red rubies and luminous blue sapphires; others contained bejewelled swords and royal crowns. Reposing in the biggest one of all, however, was a life-size statue of the Virgin and Child in solid gold.

These treasures were conveyed by ox cart and on donkeyback to the harbour of Callao, some 5 miles distant. It was almost deserted, most ships having fled from the rebel fleet, which lay at anchor within eyeshot, held at bay by the only remaining Spanish warship, the mighty *Esmeralda,* which would defend Lima to the last cannon ball. That vessel apart, there was only the *Mary Dear,* a small British brig that was speedy and manoeuvrable enough to evade the Chilean fleet. Her captain, William Thompson, was known along the coasts of South America as a capable and dependable trader – and that was what he might have remained, had not one of the most valuable treasures ever seen by human eye been conveyed aboard his ship and its custody positively enforced on him.

The Spanish grandees instructed Captain Thompson to head for the open sea and cruise beyond the horizon. If Lima fell into rebel hands he was to make for the safe haven of Panama; if not, he was to return to Lima. Thompson and his 14-man crew carried out the first part of their mission with alacrity: the *Mary Dear* and her precious cargo vanished over skyline, but they never reappeared, neither on the horizon nor off Lima or Panama. Whatever the truth – whether proximity to so much gold caused the crew to mutiny and coerce their captain into turning pirate, or whether Thompson himself succumbed to temptation – the handful of Spanish soldiers and monks who were escorting the treasure had their throats cut and were thrown overboard. After that, the *Mary Dear* disappeared into the vast expanse of the Pacific Ocean.

But where did the ship go? It is to be assumed that Captain Thompson and his mate headed for an uninhabited island named Cocos Island, ferried the treasure ashore by dinghy and buried it in a secret but readily accessible spot. It is further to be assumed that, having completed their work, they sailed eastwards to the South American mainland, and that shortly before the coast came in sight Captain Thompson ordered his men into the boats and set the ship ablaze. The *Mary Dear* was now an outlawed vessel. Thompson could not have taken her into any harbour in the world without being promptly arrested by the authorities. So he and his men rowed for the mainland and were captured off Costa Rica by a Spanish frigate. Taken back to Lima, they reported that the *Mary Dear* had got into difficulties and gone to the bottom with her precious cargo.

The plan was a good one, but it didn't work. Why not? Because the mortal remains of the murdered men-at-arms and monks had since been washed ashore. Death by natural causes was precluded by the gashes in their throats and the obvious fact that they had all been killed at the same time. The helmsman, boatswain, ship's cook, ship's carpenter and nine seamen were speedily tortured into a unanimous and extremely convincing confession: they had buried the treasure on an island named Cocos Island. As to where in God's wide world the island was, however, they couldn't say because none of them could read or write, far less navigate. Only Captain Thompson and the mate knew the island's longitude and latitude, so they alone could reveal where the treasure was buried. In view of this, the Spanish viceroy hanged the 13 sailors but granted Thompson and his mate a temporary reprieve.

Some weeks later the two pirates guided a Spanish expeditionary ship 1,000 miles north-westwards to Cocos Island. They were scarcely ashore when they dived into the bushes. The Spaniards, who failed to find them despite their best efforts, soon grew tired of conducting a manhunt in a rat-infested jungle, and when supplies ran short after a few days their captain left hostile Nature to carry out sentence of death on Thompson and his mate. He returned to the ship with his men and sailed home to Lima. In the ensuing months the viceroy dispatched at least two more well-armed expeditions to Cocos Island with orders to find the pirates and recover the treasure. They were unsuccessful.

Thompson and the mate stuck it out on the island for six months. Then the British whaler *Captain* appeared on the horizon and put in to take on water. Her captain, who believed the two men's story that they were innocent castaways, took them on board and put them ashore on the American mainland. Thereafter they vanished without trace for over 20 years.

In 1845, however, a man named Thompson lay dying at St John's in Newfoundland. Whether or not he was the former captain of the *Mary Dear*, no one can say for sure, but seated at his bedside was a youth named John Keating to whom, with his dying breaths, Thompson is said to have whispered the whereabouts of the Lima Treasure on Cocos Island. On the basis of this information Keating drew a map: the original of the hundreds of buried treasure maps that have been in circulation since then.

What happened after that is shrouded in myth. Many people claim that John Keating chartered a ship in partnership with a man named Bogue, rounded Cape Horn and got to Cocos Island, where he actually discovered a cave filled with gold and precious stones. He then sailed home to St John's laden with Spanish doubloons variously valued at $7,000, $40,000 or even $100,000, but not before – versions of the story differ on this point – shooting Bogue, throwing him overboard or burying him alive in the treasure cave, in which case Bogue's skeleton would be guarding the hoard to this day. Others claim that Keating paid two more visits to Cocos Island. Immensely wealthy by now, he purchased a large estate and a yacht, in which he was wrecked off Codroy Village in 1868. In gratitude to his coxswain, Nicholas Fitzgerald, who had saved his life, he allegedly told him the secret of the treasure island. However, those who came into possession of a treasure map are said to have included John Keating's son-in-law and his young wife and her lover, likewise the latter's brother and son, and, after Keating's death, his widow's new husband.

Because more and more of those who heard the original story took more and more people into their confidence, the mysterious tale spread rapidly in the middle of the nineteenth century. Nobody knows how many adventurers armed with treasure maps set off on the long and costly voyage to Cocos Island. People would sometimes shut up their houses and disappear into the blue. Many were never seen again, others came home after weeks or months with their tails between their legs, and still others boasted of the treasures they'd found but been compelled by adverse circumstances to leave behind. A few resisted temptation and stayed at home, where they prospered. Among them was the gallant coxswain who had saved Keating from drowning, Nicholas Fitzgerald, who spent his life fishing for cod off Newfoundland. In 1870, having got into difficulties at sea and been rescued by Admiral Curzon-Howe, he gave the latter the treasure map in token of his gratitude. Curzon-Howe – and this is also a matter of record – passed the map to Sir Malcolm Campbell, the famous British racing driver. Campbell spent many hundreds of thousands of dollars on fitting out an expedition that dropped anchor in Chatham Bay on 27 February 1926, only to depart, empty-handed, three months later. However, he did go down in history as probably the first treasure-hunter to have considered using metal detectors. In order to test the devices he had ordered, he buried an assortment of motor parts and spare wheels in the extensive grounds in front of his garage – where they remain to this day because the metal detectors were not sufficiently well developed.

Hundreds of treasure maps, letters and sketches have since come to light, having allegedly been gathering dust for decades in desks, behind paintings or in forgotten bookcases. All are claimed to be genuine, or at least genuine copies of originals formerly in the possession of Thompson, Keating, Bogue or Fitzgerald. What is fairly certain is that not a year has gone by since 1850 without some treasure-hunter toiling away on Cocos Island, and there cannot have been a day since then on which someone, somewhere in the world, has not believed himself to be in possession of highly secret information leading straight to the pirate treasure. Nobody knows how many hundreds of vessels have undertaken the voyage to Cocos Island and how many people have landed in Chatham or Wafer Bay, attacked the beach with picks and shovels, got bitten by mosquitoes and ants, and departed after a few days, weeks or months. Schoolboys have even rowed out to sea in a dinghy, made the crossing, and been rescued on the way back by the US Navy or Costa Rican coastguards. Wealthy yacht owners have often treated themselves to a little excitement between spells on the bathing beaches of Acapulco and Tahiti. Lone cranks have had themselves put ashore on the island and spent a while scanning the beaches with dowsing rods or pendulums. On one occasion a German medium named Margo Schneider is said to have gone there to establish contact with the spirit of Benito Bonito. Others have pursued their quest for the treasure in a seriously scientific manner, equipped with novel devices employing infra-red, ultrasound and electromagnetism, only to become hopelessly lost in the jungle's liana thickets. Other treasure-hunters employed dozens of Indio farm labourers to wield picks and shovels for them. Later on, American bulldozers and sticks of dynamite were brought into play. When two or three ships were anchored in Chatham Bay at the same time, as sometimes happened, search parties armed with conflicting treasure maps fought each other on the beach, blasted holes in the ground, sent fragments of rock flying about their competitors' ears, and threatened each other with knives and guns.

Finally, there were the pinstriped adventurers who founded companies with promising names like 'Cocos Expedition' (San Francisco, 1854), 'Hidden Treasure Company' (New York, 1873), 'Clayton Metalphone Ltd' (Vancouver, 1931), or 'Treasure Recovery Ltd' (London, 1934). Many of them actually fitted out expeditions and dispatched ships to Cocos Island; others never left the safety of their deep pile carpets and well heated boardrooms. The shares in all these companies were, by their very nature, extremely volatile. As a rule they steadily declined in value the longer no treasure came to light, but it could sometimes happen that very interesting articles appeared in the press or intriguing rumours went the rounds in stock market circles, whereupon the shares would soar to dizzy heights, only to nosedive because some shrewd and prescient operator had dumped a substantial holding.

On Wednesday, 1 December 1897, for example, the *New York Times* published the following report:

It is believed that by this time the $30,000,000 treasure of Cocos Island is safe on board the British cruiser *Amphion.* This is indicated by the news brought from Guatemala by the United States gunboat *Alert.* [...] It seems that when Admiral Pallister went to the island with the flagship in October he landed a party of men, and, guided by a man named Harford, they commenced digging in a certain spot. At a depth of about six feet they uncovered a large square slab of granite that had once borne some sort of an inscription. Great difficulty was experienced in the excavation, as the hole filled with water almost as fast as it could be taken out. A tackle was rigged, and the block of granite removed, disclosing the entrance to a sort of tunnel, the walls of which caved in, completely filling up the hole and almost burying a number of the exploring party. On the following day a blast was put in above the first excavation, but this only had the effect of complicating the difficulty.[2]

On 13 March 1898, a good three months later, the *New York Times* briefly reported that, according to a letter from a sailor aboard the *Amphion,* the allegedly successful hunt for treasure on Cocos Island had, after all, turned out to be fruitless. The men had dug for ten days and found nothing.

High hopes were dashed again and again, giving way to dire disappointment, and the oldest of friends became the bitterest of foes. Countless men sacrificed their physical and mental health, their financial resources and the best years of their lives to this speck in the Pacific. The happiest treasure-seekers were those who only went there for fun. One of them was US President Franklin Delano Roosevelt. On Wednesday, 9 October 1935, while cruising in the USS *Houston,* he gave the members of his entourage permission to go digging on Cocos Island for an hour or two. The president, who had contracted polio at the age of 39 and was paralysed from the waist down, remained on board and did some fishing while they were ashore. The 132-pound swordfish he caught was kept on ice and forwarded to Washington, where he had it stuffed and hung on a White House wall.

In 1968 the government of Costa Rica decided to cease issuing permits to treasure-hunters and dispatched a squad of national guardsmen to guard the island, but the influx of adventurers continued notwithstanding. Many employed trawlermen or lobster fishermen to convey them to the unguarded south coast and swam ashore;

others purchased special permits at great expense, and many secured access to the island by posing as innocent skin divers, ornithologists or botanists. In the 1960s it occurred to three young Frenchmen that the treasure might not be hidden in either of the two navigable bays but among the perilous basalt cliffs at the other end of the island. In 1978 a Costa Rican soldier discovered the wreck of a US Air Force bomber in the middle of the jungle, where it had lain undiscovered since 1943. In December 1980 the German corrugated-cardboard manufacturer Richard Gissler, who had inherited a treasure map from his great-uncle August Gissler, spent four days on the island accompanied by his daughter Claudia. In 1982 the Munich adventurer Reinhold Ostler arrived with three friends and a ton and a half of baggage, much of it consisting of a thousand cans of beer donated by a Munich brewery, but their metal detectors proved of little avail. Although the industry had developed some extremely reliable and expensive equipment since Sir Malcolm Campbell's day, hordes of treasure-hunters had left behind so many pickaxes, shovels and empty cans in the relevant area that pieces of metal were discovered every step of the way.

Today the area bordering Chatham Bay and Wafer Bay is littered with mysterious signs: enigmatic notches on centuries-old trees, little arrows on rocks and crosses on weather-worn ships' timbers. In the jungle, treasure-hunters have dug hundreds of pits many feet deep, some of them so densely overgrown that the unwary can easily fall in and break a leg. On the edge of the jungle are huts in every stage of dilapidation, on the beaches few stones bigger than a pebble on which some unsuccessful treasure-hunter has neglected to immortalize his name.

Treasure Island

WHILE WAITING FOR FANNY to obtain her divorce, Louis hung around the San Francisco waterfront for week after week, coughing, plagued by bouts of fever and suffering agonies with his bad teeth. Christmas Eve he spent by himself in a cheap restaurant. For four whole days he didn't exchange a word with anyone except his landlady. It would be another two years before he wrote *Treasure Island,* and his financial prospects were bleak. His money was running out fast, no more could be expected, and there was no hope of assistance from his puritanical parents. Indeed, it was more likely that they would disinherit him for living in sin with a married woman. 'I am glad they mean to disinherit me. [...] I always had doubts about inherited money and this clears me of that forever.'[1]

Louis reduced his daily expenditure on food from 45 to 25 cents. He made renewed job applications to newspaper offices. He started work on a novel entitled 'What Was on the Slate' but didn't get far with it. Eventually he wrote to his friend Charles Baxter in Edinburgh asking him to sell all his books and send the proceeds to California.

In January 1880 Fanny's marriage to Samuel Osbourne was dissolved at last, enabling Louis to marry her. However, it was at this juncture that he began to cough up blood for the first time. He could hardly speak, his mouth was so full of it. The doctor, who was hurriedly sent for, diagnosed tuberculosis in its terminal stage – a death sentence which the sick man greeted with surprising equanimity. 'I know I am on my trial; if I can keep well next winter I have every reason to hope the best; but on the other hand, I may very well never see next spring. In view of this, I am all the more anxious she should see my father and mother; they are well off, thank God; and even suppose that I die, Fanny will be better off than she had much chance of being otherwise.'[2]

But then came spring 1880, and all turned out well. Back home in Scotland, Louis's parents must have gathered from a newspaper report that their only son was laid up with a dangerous disease. They were horrified. 'Our letters and the twenty pounds we sent you have been returned from New York,' his father wrote. His mother scolded him for taking 'such risks' with his health, advised her impoverished son to fortify himself by drinking plenty of champagne, and informed him that he would lack for nothing 'so long as we still have a penny'. As for their future daughter-in-law, Margaret and Thomas Stevenson's verdict on her was considerably milder now that she had obtained a divorce – not in Edinburgh, God be praised, but thousands of miles away in California – and was, so to speak, single once more. Mrs Stevenson informed Louis that his bride would be welcome in her home. His father drew attention to the fact that it would be proper to leave as long an interval as possible between her divorce and remarriage. Last but not least, he informed Louis by telegram that he would be making him an annual allowance of £250, starting at once, and that part-payment was already on its way.

Louis's first step was to have all his decaying teeth extracted and replaced with dentures. He bought two plain silver wedding rings and applied for a marriage licence. He also rented decent accommodation for Fanny and Lloyd and their horses and informed Samuel Osbourne that he was released from all his financial obligations. One spring evening at the beginning of May he and Fanny attended a performance of *The Pirates of Penzance,* which was playing to full houses at the Bush Street Theater. A few weeks later, on 19 May 1880, Robert Louis Stevenson and Frances Mathilda Osbourne, née Vandegrift, were married at the home of the Reverend William Scott, 521 Post Street. The minister was a Scottish Presbyterian and a man after Louis's heart in other respects as well. In his youth he had fought against the Black Hawk Indians as a chaplain under Abraham Lincoln. He had then earned a living for many years as a rodeo rider in Tennessee before settling in San Francisco in 1852, where he had built two churches and written 11 religious books. One surmises that the worldly-wise cleric must have taken a liking to the bridal pair, who might almost have passed for mother and son, or that he at least took an indulgent view of their union. When completing the awkward 'marital status' entry on the marriage certificate he preserved the bride from the stigma of 'divorced' – possibly at her express request – and tactfully wrote 'widow'. It is also possible that Fanny or Louis dictated the marriage announcement in the newspapers. At all events, the *Oakland Tribune* of 22 May 1880 referred to the bride as 'Miss Fannie Osbourne, of Oakland'.

Sam Osbourne remained on friendly terms with Fanny and the children after the divorce. His weekly letters to Lloyd, who was still a minor, were affectionate in tone and often enquired how Fanny was getting on. In San Francisco three years later he married a girl named Rebecca Paul, whom he called 'Pauly'. He continued to earn his living as a court clerk until, on 28 March 1887, he put on his hat and coat to go to work, asked Pauly, when saying goodbye to her on the doorstep, to make lunch for them both – and never reappeared. His disappearance caused a stir in the press. Many people suspected that he had been having an affair, others that he had been shanghaied, and someone even claimed he had been seen in Africa. Finally, a few months later, all such rumours were laid to rest by the discovery on the beach of a bedraggled bundle of clothes. Although no one could say for sure that they had belonged to Samuel Osbourne, his friends were convinced that the lifelong depressive had drowned himself.

Fanny and Louis's wedding was the prelude to a ten-year odyssey that took them halfway round the globe from one tuberculosis sanatorium to the next, from Scotland twice to the Alps and back, to the South of France and all the way across North America. They were to remain constantly on the move until that morning in December 1889 when the *Equator* reached the shores of Samoa.

Every day of their married life was coloured by Louis's disease and Fanny's strict maternal solicitude. No one who saw them ever remarked that they were a carefree loving couple linked by ties of affection or erotic passion. On the other hand, there is no evidence of any marital dispute that lasted longer than a day or a night, for the disparate pair were devoted to each other: Louis the self-centred artist whose state of health governed the life of the entire family, but who submissively bowed to his wife's wishes in minor, everyday matters; and Fanny the domineering matron who humbly devoted herself to keeping her frail young husband alive. She prescribed his diet, negotiated with his doctors, decided on visits to this health resort or that. She became furious if his friends overstayed their welcome in the evenings and made sure he wrapped up warm when leaving the house. Only one thing never occurred to her, being a heavy smoker herself: that it might be harmful to his diseased respiratory organs to chain-smoke cigarettes all year round from early in the morning until late at night.

In May 1880, because Louis's lungs were rattling alarmingly, Fanny decided that it would not be a good thing to spend their honeymoon in the misty sea air of San Francisco. Louis was too weak to travel far and hadn't enough money for a stay at the nearby hot springs of Calistoga, at the foot of Mount Helena. So he, Fanny and Lloyd spent two months living free of charge in an abandoned silver mine further up the mountain. It was five or ten years since the last miners had moved out. What remained was a deep canyon, a breathtaking view, and a hut on a wooden platform perched on the hillside. Rotting timbers and rusty pieces of iron lay around everywhere, and the grass concealed rails that led to ruined shafts pervaded by cool, moist currents of air. The hut was littered with old clothes, broken tools and rickety furniture. Fanny set to work at once. With housewifely determination she put things back in their places, nailed things together again, hung things on the wall, and swept and washed and scrubbed away until the hut was relatively habitable. Louis, who had grown up in a household full of maidservants, was no great help. After giving the place the once-over he pulled out a poison oak that had grown up through the floorboards. Then, leaving everything else to his wife, he went off to look around. He delightedly recorded in his notebook that there were 'billy goats, bears and rattlesnakes' in the area.

Louis recovered quickly in the hot, dry mountain air. He pored over his manuscripts for four or five hours a day, but without producing much. Fanny made sure he didn't overdo it and forbade him to go for walks. He coughed less from day to day, ate more and probably put on some weight. 'I am truly better,' he wrote to his mother on 30 June. 'I am allowed to do nothing; never leave our little platform in the canyon, nor do a stroke of work.'[3] A few days later Fanny reported to her mother-in-law: 'As to my dear boy's appearance, he improves every day in the most wonderful way, so that I fancy by the time you see him you will hardly know that he has ever been ill at all. I do try to take care of him; the old doctor insists that my nursing saved him.'[4]

Finally, at the end of July, Louis, Fanny and Lloyd set off on the long journey to Scotland. Thanks to the Stevensons' munificence they travelled by first-class sleeping car from San Francisco to New York and crossed the Atlantic on the top deck of the *City of Chester*. On 17 August 1880, exactly one year and ten days since his departure on board the *Devonia*, Louis was back home. Thomas and Margaret Stevenson were standing on the quayside at Liverpool, ready to give him a reconciliatory embrace.

A year later came the day on which Louis would go down in the annals of world literature. He was sitting beside the fire in a cottage at Braemar in the Scottish Highlands which his parents had rented for the summer, with a scarf around his neck and his legs swathed in a rug. 'Here I am in my native land, being gently blown and hailed upon, and sitting nearer and nearer to the fire.' [5] In the summer of 1881, which was exceptionally wet even by Scottish standards, his health had dramatically deteriorated once more. The doctor had forbidden him to go outside in such weather. He sat obediently beside the fire for week after week, writing and reading, reading and writing. Then he had had a haemorrhage and the doctor had forbidden him to utter a word before lunch. If he had something important to say he communicated it in a sign language of his own devising, so the house was silent. Fanny and his mother took care of the housework. Thomas Stevenson was out during the day, and Lloyd, by now a lanky youngster of 12, whiled away the time with pencil and watercolours. The only really active member of the household was a little brown Skye terrier, a gift to Louis from his friend Walter Simpson. The dog was cute, lively and ill-behaved. Fanny originally named it Walter after the donor, but it later became variously known as Woggle, Woggs, Woggy, Watty or Wiggs.

It must have been on a day towards the end of August 1881 when Louis borrowed pencil and paper from Lloyd and made a drawing of his own. It was a map of a small, uninhabited island, 'about nine miles long and five across, shaped, you might say, like a fat dragon standing up, and had two fine, land-locked harbours, and a hill in the centre part marked "The Spy-glass".' [6] A three-masted schooner lay at anchor in a bay. To the west and south, where strong currents rendered a landing almost impossible, waves broke against steep grey cliffs overlooked by dense jungle. Using Lloyd's watercolours, Louis painted the sea blue, the jungle green and the ship's timbers brown. Then he made a red cross and wrote beside it, in neat little lettering, 'Main treasure here'. Above his painting he wrote 'Treasure Island'.

As I paused upon my map of "Treasure Island", the future character of the book began to appear there visibly among imaginary woods; and their brown faces and bright weapons peeped out upon me from unexpected quarters, as they passed to and fro, fighting and hunting treasure, on these few square inches of a flat projection. The next thing I knew, I had some papers before me and was writing out a list of chapters.[7]

That day, Louis sat down and wrote the first chapter, which he read to Lloyd after supper. The next day he wrote the second chapter and read that, too, aloud after supper. Chapter Three followed the day after that. Fanny later recalled that the whole thing had simply been meant to entertain a boy condemned by bad weather to inactivity indoors. Before long, however, Louis noticed that another, considerably older boy was hanging on his every word. 'My father caught fire at once with all the romance and childishness of his original nature. [...] He not only heard with delight the daily chapter, but set himself to collaborate.' Thomas Stevenson listed the contents of Billy Bones's chest, christened Captain Flint's old ship *Walrus,* and suggested the scene in which the hero of the story, 12-year-old Jim Hawkins, overhears the pirates plotting while hidden in an apple barrel.

The ensuing days in rainy Braemar were happy ones. Louis's friends Sidney Colvin and the writer Edmund Gosse happened to be staying there at the time, and because the occupants of the cottage were so well known to each other they soon evolved an agreeable daily routine – though all present took it for granted that its focus was the literary invalid. The mornings Louis invariably spent in bed. Since he was not allowed to speak before lunch, Colvin and Gosse took it in turns to play chess with him. If he tired of the game he would push the board aside and request his writing things. Then no one could disturb him until supper-time. After supper everyone gathered in the sitting room and Louis read them what he had written during the day. Many years later, Edmund Gosse wrote that he could not remember anything more pleasurable than those chilly nights in Braemar, when the wind howled outside, hail rattled against the window panes and Louis read his budding novel aloud by the light of an oil lamp, raising his voice and gesticulating whenever he came to a dramatic passage.

So the story made rapid headway. In the first chapter Billy Bones, the old sea dog, appears on the scene. In the second Jim Hawkins finds the treasure map. In the tenth Jim sets sail with the map, heading south-west, and in the 12th, after a long voyage, Treasure Island's precipitous, conical shape looms up out of the mist. In the 13th chapter the treasure-hunters go ashore, in the 14th the first murder occurs, the 15th introduces Ben Gunn, who has spent three years of his life marooned alone on the island, and then, and then ... Quite suddenly, Robert Louis Stevenson had run out of ideas. 'Fifteen days I stuck it, and turned out fifteen chapters; and then, in the early paragraphs of the sixteenth, ignominiously lost hold. My mouth was empty; there was not one word of TREASURE ISLAND in my bosom.'[8]

Perhaps he had overtaxed himself during those first two weeks and run out of steam; perhaps he was also suffering from common or garden writer's block, which is as hard to explain as its opposite, the act of literary creation. This verbal drought was doubly unfortunate because he had already sold the story as a serial to the London children's magazine *Young Folks,* which proposed to publish the first chapter in a fortnight's time, on 1 October 1881. Louis did what many writers would have done under such circumstances: he ventured out of the house again, got drunk with his friends and made an excursion to Edinburgh. That helped a bit, but not much. He completed the 16th chapter, in which hostilities are brewing between the loyalists and the mutineers; and the 17th, in which hostilities continue to develop; and the 18th, in which someone gets killed; and the 19th and 20th, in which a lot of ammunition is expended. But he failed to regain his former one-chapter-a-day momentum, and countless readers have since felt that these chapters cause the story to mark time in a curious way.

He finally resorted to something that often helps writers in distress: a change of scene. His health had deteriorated so badly by the end of September that there were renewed fears for his survival. It was decided that he should spend the winter recuperating at Davos, as he had the year before. Together with Fanny and Lloyd, he travelled to Switzerland via Edinburgh, London and Paris, reaching Davos on the evening of 18 October.

SKIING HAD YET TO BE INTRODUCED into Switzerland in the winter of 1881. It would be another seven years before a consumptive British officer went to Davos accompanied by his Norwegian valet, who took a pair of skis with him and left them behind on their departure. When Louis, Fanny and Lloyd reached Davos after an eight-hour sleigh ride from Landquart station, the Swiss Alps were still a place of peaceful though hostile beauty, not a species of amusement park. Davos, which stood isolated amid snow-capped peaks on the bare, windy highland plateau of the Landwassertal, comprised a handful of scattered farmhouses and barns plus a few hotels and sanatoria inhabited by half-dead consumptives who followed the instructions of Carl Rüedi, the world famous expert on lung diseases, with varying degrees of compliance.

In contrast to the previous winter, when they had stayed at the Hotel Belvedere, the Stevensons put up at a chalet called Am Stein, which was situated in the lee of a massive rocky outcrop on the edge of the village. Louis was not averse to following Dr Rüedi's regimen, which prescribed – in addition to daily cold showers – the ingestion of a lot of milk, red meat and Veltliner red wine, but he rather reluctantly complied with a ban on smoking cigarettes and on doing no more than three hours' work a day. Like the rest of Rüedi's patients, he had to spend the remainder of the time resting on his balcony in a lounger or taking physical exercise, which consisted mainly of short walks up the same old beaten tracks to the larch woods. Day after day, with soldierly discipline, Louis set off on the doctor's prescribed walks, dragging Woggs, the Skye terrier, after him. He soon noticed that he always passed the same fellow patients in the same places, and that the snow was always sprinkled in the same places with the same dogs' urine, and that where the same chronic patients had had their little coughing fits the snow was sometimes sprinkled with red droplets.

The Stevensons were in a bad way for the first few weeks of their seven-month stay. Louis was coughing up blood, Fanny suffering from gallstones, and Lloyd caught influenza and broke a finger. Woggle had a painful abscess in his right ear which no one but Louis was permitted to treat. Despite all his tribulations, however, Louis's creative energy returned. One October morning a few days after his arrival he unpacked the unfinished novel and sat down to do his permitted three-hour stint – 'and behold! it flowed from me like small talk; and in a second tide of delighted industry, and again at a rate of a chapter a day, I finished TREASURE ISLAND.'[9]

He took 14 days to write the remaining 14 chapters. By the time the story ended the skeleton had made its appearance. The treasure map had proved to be worthless, the main hoard had been found in an unexpected place, and a total of 17 mutineers had lost their lives. When the *Hispaniola* weighed anchor and set sail for 'the nearest port in Spanish America', heavily laden with gold, she left the three surviving pirates to their fate on the inhospitable island. On the 15th day Louis read the whole book through again. He found it satisfactory, stuffed the manuscript into an envelope and posted it off to London. On 22 November 1881 the publisher sent him a fee of £30.

IT GOES WITHOUT SAYING that the snowy Swiss Alps provide no clue to whether Robert Louis Stevenson had a real island in mind. He doubtless saw Alpine choughs and horse-drawn sleighs in Davos, but no parrots or pirate ships, and the panorama visible from his balcony at Am Stein – the Rhaetikon in the north, the Piz d'Aela, Tinzenhorn and Piz Michel in the south – bore no resemblance to a tropical island. However, one minor detail is worth mentioning: in the ensuing months, Louis bestowed a new name on his dog Woggle, which had now been accompanying the family everywhere for some two years. It was an unusual thing to do, because people find it hard to forget a familiar name and accustom themselves to a new one. Despite this, Woggle suddenly ceased to be Woggle, or Woggs, Woggy, Watty or Wiggs and became Bogue.[10]

Apart from being a rare name in the English-speaking world, Bogue was a far from conventional appellation for a 19th-century Skye terrier. Why Louis should have taken the trouble to enforce this new name on Fanny, Lloyd and the rechristened animal itself will always remain his secret. It cannot have been intended as a tribute to some friend or relative; as far as we know, Louis never had anything to do with anyone called Bogue. No such name appears in any Davos visitors' book, nor is it the name of any fictional character in the Stevenson oeuvre. The only Bogue to be found anywhere crops up in connection with a small volcanic island off the coast of Costa Rica. Even though Louis swore again and again that *Treasure Island* had no basis in fact, the name he gave his dog can only be construed as an indication that he was well acquainted with the story of Cocos Island. For Bogue, as we have seen, was the name of the man whose partnership with the treasure-hunter John Keating cost him his life when he was either shot, thrown overboard, or buried alive in the treasure cave itself, and whose skeleton may – just possibly – be guarding the Lima Treasure to this day.

The frisky little Skye terrier bore its new name for another four years. In the spring of 1885, while confined to a veterinary hospital in Bournemouth, Bogue attacked a considerably bigger inmate and paid for this temerity with his life. Fanny, Lloyd and Louis were inconsolable. They never acquired another dog.

I'll Hope for the Best ...

MOST ADVENTURERS AND TREASURE-HUNTERS on Cocos Island stuck it out for a few days only, some for three or four weeks, and just a handful for months. But one of them beat all the rest hands down, not in terms of success but for sheer perseverance and determination.

It may not have been entirely fortuitous that it was a German who realized that looking for treasure should be a methodical, not a random procedure. The German's name was August Gissler, and he was a professional sailor. He was 31 years old when he first set foot on Cocos Island in the autumn of 1888, and 67 years had elapsed since the disappearance of the Lima Treasure. It was 40 years since the first treasure maps had come into circulation and nine years since Robert Louis Stevenson had read of the unsuccessful expeditions to Cocos Island in the *San Francisco Call*. However, August Gissler was unaware of this when he came into possession of a treasure map. He believed that his map was unique and genuine. By the time he realized his mistake he could not admit to it; he devoted nearly 20 years of his life to searching for treasure on Cocos Island.

August Gissler was born on 19 September 1857 at Remscheid, near Solingen, the third of 11 children of a middle-class knife manufacturer. Gissler Snr wanted his sons to take over the firm some day and, in the far distant future, to hand it on to their own sons. His eldest son Hermann* not only fulfilled that hope but exceeded it; August,

---

*Hermann Gissler (1856–1919) founded the firm Gissler & Pass of Jülich, West Germany's oldest and biggest manufacturer of corrugated cardboard, which is now headed by Thomas Gissler-Weber, a member of the fourth generation.

the next in line, did not. At the age of 20 or so, whether he was averse to being a junior partner in the family firm and playing second fiddle to his elder brother, or whether he simply shrank from spending a lifetime as a Remscheid businessman, he vanished overnight. The family did not hear of him again for ten years. It appears that, after spending some time at sea, he landed in Hawaii and bought a small sugar plantation next to that of another German immigrant named Barthels. Gissler led a quiet, frugal, hard-working life in his fields. He spent his Sundays at the home of Barthels, who was married to a Hawaiian woman and had raised a family with her. One Sunday, Barthels showed Gissler a treasure map said to have belonged to his Hawaiian father-in-law, who had allegedly been a seaman in his youth. This map was of a small island where the Lima Treasure was said to be buried at a depth of 6 feet in a small bay in the north-west of the island.

August Gissler, who believed every word, was so fired with enthusiasm that he dropped everything and sold his plantation. On 18 May 1888 he sailed for San Francisco accompanied by Barthels and the latter's 11-year-old son, his intention being to purchase a vessel that would convey them the 2,485 miles along the west coast of America to Cocos Island. It would have to be seaworthy and capable of being handled by two men and an 11-year-old boy, because the treasure-hunters wanted to avoid hiring any strangers for security reasons. Gissler spent seven weeks combing San Francisco harbour for suitable vessels, but in vain. Either they required a considerably bigger crew, or their capacity was insufficient, or they were not seaworthy enough.

Quite by chance, August Gissler's and Robert Louis Stevenson's paths crossed at this time. Louis spent the period 7–28 June 1888 in San Francisco before going aboard the *Casco* and setting off on the South Seas odyssey that was to end in Samoa 18 months later. Gissler arrived on 3 June and remained there until the end of July, but there is no indication that the two men were aware of each other's presence.

Gissler, Barthels and the boy eventually travelled by steamer to Costa Rica, where they landed at Puntarenas, the country's principal port. Although they were now only 310 miles from their goal, Gissler discovered to his disappointment that the 'secret' of Cocos Island had long ceased to be one. 'Several expeditions have already been there to look for it,' he wrote in a long (and rather disjointed) letter to his family in Remscheid:

Before he died in the hospital at New Bedford, an old sailor is supposed to have said that he was one of the pirates, and that the gold lies buried on Cocos Island. [...] Then we heard from people after the gold that they had a man on board who said he knew where the gold was, but when they got there he couldn't find it, so after three weeks they sailed away and tried to sell the schooner in Panama, but they failed and then they came to Puntarenas. Now the seamen pointed on the map to where they had already dug. They say there are holes there big enough to bury a house in, and then they asked me where we proposed to dig. I showed them nearby, then they said that I should save myself the trouble because that was more or less the place where they themselves had looked, and for roughly half a mile around everything has been dug up, because that is where the pirate village used to be. But our plan shows the other side of the island, so I have more faith in it. Then I asked the people what the other place looks like. They said it was all overgrown with creeper, and one can't land on that side, it's all steep rocks. There's absolutely no doubt that the gold is on the island, because if such masses were found it would become known. There's supposed to be 20 to 25 million dollars' worth, and that couldn't be kept secret. Whether we will find it is a big question. I'll hope for the best, and then no member of our family will ever have to work again, that much is certain.[1]

Under the circumstances, Gissler and Barthels should sensibly have given up and gone home. Barthels did just that. He shipped himself and his son back to San Francisco and returned to his Hawaiian plantation, leaving the treasure map behind with August Gissler, who had resolved to stay. To him, the obvious fact that Puntarenas harbour was swarming with treasure-hunters was simply additional proof of the treasure's existence. If it had not been found yet, this could only mean that everyone had been looking in the wrong place. A week after Barthels left, a Swedish schooner put in with a cargo of cedarwood bound for Chile. The captain was short of six hands. August Gissler offered to sign on provided the ship made an intermediate two-week stop at Cocos Island.

'We set sail on 19 September, my birthday, but had very little wind. We came within sight of Cocos Island, but contrary wind and currents drove us back into the Bay of Panama. We tried for about twelve days after that, always within sight of land, but could get no closer because the ship was too big for our crew. I wanted to try notwithstanding, but the captain said he could delay no longer, he had to get to Valparaiso and was short of supplies. But he had a brother in Valparaiso, a former sea captain who, he said, had a few ships of his own. He would provide a ship, and we could take the time to remain on the island for a few months. So after a voyage we arrived at the beginning of December ...

August Gissler's 73 days at sea had given him ample time in which to plan his future course of action. He now realized that his original scheme – to sail to Cocos Island as surreptitiously as possible, unearth the treasure in short order, and sneak off with equal rapidity – could not be implemented. To have any prospect of success the expedition would have to be planned on a far bigger scale. The ship had to be not only seaworthy but capacious enough to transport many tons of gold and precious stones. This would require a crew of at least ten men, all of whom would have to be fed and paid. But August Gissler had no money, so he persuaded 14 Valparaiso merchants and civil servants to set up a company with him.

To cover the ship's additional expenses we have sold shares to a value of 3,000 dollars. For every 100 dollars the people will get 20,000 dollars if we find it; otherwise they will lose their money. Most of the money has been subscribed by the bigger merchants; a German firm, 'Benaro', has subscribed 400 dollars. Well, as I say, if all goes well we're made; if not, we must accept the fact. No need to let this be known outside the family; you can always do so when we've found it.

Gissler chartered the *Wilhelmina,* a barque of 350 tons. All 14 shareholders were on board when she sailed. In the middle of March 1889 the *Wilhelmina* dropped anchor in Chatham Bay and August Gissler at last set foot on Cocos Island for the first time. He took a preliminary look round and came back on board, where he spread out his treasure map and compared it with the lie of the land. The two mountains east and west of the anchorage were marked on the map, and lines leading from their summits intersected at a point a few hundred yards inland. Written beside this, in Spanish, were the words, 'Here we buried a very valuable treasure in 1821. After we had buried the treasure we planted a coconut palm above it and determined the position by compass. The treasure lies N.E. by E.½E. from the eastern mountain and N.10 deg. from the western mountain.'

August Gissler and his fellow shareholders went ashore, pitched their tents and proceeded to cut paths through the bush. Having fought their way to the two lines' point of intersection, they optimistically felled the palm tree growing above it and proceeded to dig in the steamy heat of the rainforest. They cut down a second palm tree and dug a second hole, then a third and a fourth and a fifth. It rained incessantly, day and night. After a month, by which time their supplies were running low, ten of the 14 shareholders had had enough and wanted to go home. The other four, who included August Gissler, decided to stay. The *Wilhelmina*'s remaining stores were divided into 14 equal parts, four of which were taken ashore. The ten disheartened treasure-hunters promised to return within three months, bringing fresh supplies.

Meanwhile, the four stalwarts continued to excavate the site of every coconut palm to be found anywhere near the point of intersection, spreading their net ever wider. One day, when they stopped digging long enough to go hunting pigs, they came across the ruins of a small wooden shack overgrown with creeper. Hanging on the door was a notice in English and Spanish: 'On 31 January 1884 Captain Schwers, commanding the steamship *Neko,* found this island uninhabited and took possession of it in the name of the German Emperor.' The treasure-hunters stripped the shack of vegetation and moved in.

The *Wilhelmina* did not return. After six months Gissler and his companions began to fear that the other shareholders had abandoned them, so they built a boat out of tree trunks and lianas, intending to sail it back to the mainland. In September 1889, however, just as they were about to set off, the other shareholders reappeared bringing ample supplies of tools and provisions. They all set to work once more, felling and digging, felling and digging. After another three months Gissler saw sense and returned to Valparaiso with all hands.

But not for long. By October 1890 he had convinced his shareholders of the need to mount another expedition. Even more generously equipped with tools and provisions than before, he made his second landing in Wafer Bay. This time the men persevered for four months. They were then forced to concede that their treasure map did not give a precise indication of the treasure's hiding-place. For his part, August Gissler came to an important conclusion: he mustn't persist in repeating his predecessors' mistakes. It was no use continuing to dig at random on the strength of dubious treasure maps and unreliable reports. The only sensible method would be to expand the search outwards in concentric circles, if necessary all the way across the island. Cocos Island was minute compared to the immensity of the Pacific, but it must have seemed gigantic to a man who set out to excavate its entire surface to a depth of several feet with pick and shovel. For that he would need far more time than even the best-equipped expedition had at its disposal. August Gissler resolved to settle on Cocos Island for the rest of his days.

He sailed back to Puntarenas and travelled on to San José, the Costa Rican capital, to obtain government permission to establish an agricultural colony on Cocos Island. In July 1891 he was granted this by President José Joaquin Rodriguez Zeledón on condition that he settle 50 German families on the island. The president also handed him a treasure map of Cocos Island that had come into the government's possession by some unknown means. Although quite similar in appearance to Gissler's map, it indicated a hiding-place closer to the beach.

In the winter of 1891/2 August Gissler travelled to Germany to recruit 50 families and new investors. However, no one in his native land shared his enthusiasm for pirate treasure and fertile volcanic islands. Having returned to Puntarenas via New York and San Francisco after four abortive months, he set off on his third expedition to Cocos Island. Even if no settlers were prepared to follow him, he decided to take another gamble and try his luck with the Costa Rican government's treasure map.

The new excavation site was located on the shingly beach about 50 feet from the high-water line. Gissler dug down until water seeped in from all sides and the walls collapsed. He waited for the tide to go out and went on digging. He dammed a stream near the site and diverted it into the sea. With the greatest difficulty, he dug down a good 6 feet 6 inches until he hit ground-water and could dig no deeper. On the reasonable assumption that the pirates must have encountered the same insurmountable problems when hiding the treasure, and that it could not be buried any deeper, he dug a second hole immediately beside the first, followed by a third and a fourth and a fifth. After a month, when he had dug up most of the beach, he abandoned the struggle.

It took August Gissler five days to sail back to the mainland – time enough for him to swallow his disappointment and seize upon the smallest crumb of hope. This presented itself immediately after he landed at Puntarenas. According to an article in the *New York Herald,* a certain Mr Young of Boston was a son-in-law of John Keating and claimed to have information regarding the whereabouts of the Lima Treasure. Gissler promptly set off on the 3,728-mile journey to Boston, where he paid Mr Young $700 for his information – and saw at a glance that his map was no use. Despite this, he returned to Puntarenas and got the Pacific mailboat to land him on Cocos Island, whence it undertook to pick him up in two weeks' time.

It didn't take Gissler two weeks to convince himself of the use-lessness of Mr Young's treasure map. It was now five years since he had left his sugar cane plantation in Hawaii. He had used up all his savings long ago, likewise his shareholders' capital, and all he had hitherto discovered on Cocos Island were numerous places where the treasure certainly *wasn't*.

On 8 May 1894, when Costa Rica elected a young president in the person of Rafael Yglesias Castro, August Gissler obtained an audi-ence with the 32-year-old head of state. If German settlers were to be lured to the island, he told him, they must be offered land. The government should therefore grant him the western half of Cocos Island – in other words, the area in which the treasure was gener-ally assumed to be – and divide the eastern half into parcels of land for potential settlers. Although initially averse to this proposal, the president eventually agreed.[*]

Now that he was the de facto master of Cocos Island, August Gissler undertook another, more successful trip to Germany. First, he probably managed to extract some money from his elder brother, Hermann, and his sisters Alma, Emmy, Anna and Johanna. This is at least implied by the fact that he left large tracts of Cocos Island to them in his will. Secondly, he married a girl of whom nothing

---

[*]August Gissler wrote his brother Hermann a letter explaining the precise terms of the agreement: '... under this contract, if I have found the treasure by the first of January 1900, the government will give me 3,000 hectares of land on the island as my property, and to every family as much land as they have cultivated plus half as much again. There are some other people here who went to the government and wanted to look for the treasure. So I made the new contract. [...] The government claims one-third of the treasure if I find it, and then I would have to sign away so-and-so-many per cent of it to some other people. That leaves half for us. If we find something, well and good, half will be more than enough for me and you. If we find nothing, the land is definitely ours, and that'll be worth a mint of money in time to come.'

is known but her name: Clara. And, thirdly, he found six families prepared to join him in establishing a German colony on Cocos Island. The Pacific mailboat landed the settlers at Chatham Bay on 13 December 1894. They had brought timbers, planks, nails and other building materials from New York and seeds, hens, ducks and turkeys from Panama. Their first step was to build houses, clear land and plant sugar cane, bananas, vegetables and coffee. In May 1895 the colony was joined by another four families and three single men from Germany. Cocos Island was now inhabited by over 50 people – more than ever before. The government granted August Gissler Costa Rican citizenship and appointed him Governor of Cocos Island. It was also arranged that a supply ship should call at the island once a month.

The German settlers had been hoping for a better life as prosperous plantation owners in the eternal southern sun. Their daily existence on the island soon disabused them of that idea. While August Gissler dug for treasure, the men of the colony strove to grow potatoes and maize in the muddy soil and their womenfolk defended their shacks and infants against rats and insects. Within a few months the first settlers had had enough and returned to the mainland in the supply ship. Three years later the last three families departed, and because the supply ship discontinued its visits in December 1898 August and Clara Gissler spent nearly two years alone on Cocos Island. Food-stuffs, tools and ammunition either ran out or wore out. By October 1900 the situation had become so serious that Gissler built a boat with his own hands, hoisted a sail made from the sheets of his marriage bed, and navigated himself and Clara to the mainland in three days – only to return to Cocos Island not long afterwards.

IN NOVEMBER 1904 August Gissler was back in New York to welcome a party of British treasure-hunters. On that occasion the Governor of Cocos Island, by then probably on the verge of insanity, granted an interview to a *New York Times* reporter who was clearly impressed by him:

> Captain Gissler is a man of 47 years, and a breathing replica of Michael Angelo's [sic] heroic statue of Moses. His reddish beard reaches to his waist, his hair is luxuriant on a splendidly poised head, his eyes are as clear and searching as an eagle's, his nose is classic, his voice is

profoundly mellow, fitting the man to perfection. His height is 6 feet 3 inches. He is built like a wedge, as a man should be, with massive shoulders, firm hips, and an almost imperceptible embonpoint. His hand is as big as the hand of Providence and so hard that his clenched fist is used as a spike maul. 'Cocos,' said Gov. Gissler, on the eve of his departure, 'is unquestionably of volcanic origin. Our highest mountain is 2,500 feet. We have seven rivers. On one is a grand waterfall of 600 feet, and on another a cataract of 500 feet. Within 100 feet of my residence I can get a force of 2000 horse power.'

'What is the character of the soil?'

'We have sand, clay, and chocolate loam. The soil is very rich. Vegetation is abundant. The forests are magnificent. Our cedar, the white or yellow species, is plentiful and apparently grainless. It should make fine pencils.'

'What of the climate?'

'The temperature ranges between 62 and 90 degrees. We never used a fire or an overcoat, and the heat does not trouble us at all. I wear a suit of overalls the year round and am comfortable. It rains ten months of the year and occasionally we have showers in the other two. The water is the purest in the world. I never had it analyzed.'

'Any game?'

'There are many kinds of birds, but none that you would eat. They are only pretty to look at and are mostly of the parrot and cockatoo order. The woods are full of wild pigs, and when I want fresh meat I kill them. The waters are alive with fish, but tropical fish, you know, are not very edible.'

'You raise domestic animals, I suppose?'

'I did have some cattle, a few horses, sheep, and chickens, but when I came to America the time before this trip an expedition from Vancouver went down there and killed every living thing.'

'Why did your people permit that?'

'My people? I haven't any.'

'I mean your – your subjects.'

'Oh, there are no subjects. Only I and my wife live on the island.'

'And when you go away?'

'She goes with me, We leave the cattle, horses, and so forth, to take care of themselves. There is enough to eat all the time.'

'No children?'

'Not one. What would be the good of a parcel of children on Cocos Island? Only trouble. They would always want to go to the mainland.'

'Isn't your wife lonely?'

'Not where I am. She likes it down there. Besides, there is plenty to do. We both work.'

'What do you find to do?;

'Lately I have been growing tobacco. I raise 1,000 pounds to the acre on the chocolate loam, and then I have a return crop in six weeks which gives 500 pounds more. If I care to do so I can raise several crops in a year, one right after the other, up to a total of 5,000 pounds to the acre.'

'That sounds incredible, Governor.'

'But it is true. I sell my crop in Costa Rica at $1 a pound.'

'One man cannot cultivate many acres. Why don't you import some labor?'

'I took out eighteen Germans once, with their families, and thought they would raise great crops and all get rich, but in a short time they raised an insurrection instead.'

'What became of the insurrection?'

'I quelled it.'

'Tell me how.'

'I declared martial law, as Governor of the island, and with my big pistols pointed in the faces of the Germans scared them into submission. They laid down what arms they had and peace was restored. But the incident induced me to ship the whole caboodle away.'

'You are Governor, General, Colonel, and the whole army, as well as Lord High Executioner, Judge, jury, and undertaker?'

'Everything, I suppose. I have to be.'

[...]

'What are your immediate plans, Governor?'

'I am going to take out a cargo of peons to Cocos, and with them shall plant 50,000 rubber trees. [...] There is another crop in which I am interested, and that is ginseng. What is ginseng, anyway? What is it used for? I hear it can be grown to enormous profit – as much as $50,000 an acre. I shall take along some roots and try what I can do.'[2]

A few days after this interview August Gissler returned to Cocos Island accompanied by his faithful wife. We do not know if Clara shared her husband's unwavering enthusiasm. What is certain is that she never left his side throughout those years. It is equally certain that he never made a fortune out of tobacco, rubber or ginseng. The tobacco seedlings rotted, the rubber trees perished, the ginseng roots sank into the muddy soil. After a few months history repeated itself: food ran low and ammunition became sodden by the incessant downpour. In order to obtain fresh supplies from the mainland, Gissler built himself another boat and hoisted his bed sheets once more. He promised Clara he would return in six weeks at the most, but a storm drove him off course. Instead of landing at Puntarenas he was washed up on the coast of Panama, several hundred miles to the south. It took him almost six months to get back to Cocos Island. When the mailboat eventually landed him in Chatham Bay he found Clara in the best of health – despite the fact that she had fallen over and broken her arm on the day he left. She had splinted the arm quite satisfactorily with sticks and lianas, set traps with the other arm, and lived on the animals that got caught in them.

It is quite possible that August Gissler came to his senses when he saw his courageous wife standing all alone on the beach in Chatham Bay. It is equally possible that this was when he realized he had subjected her – and himself – to hardships enough. On the other hand, perhaps he was merely worried about her arm and wanted a doctor to examine it. Whatever the truth, August and Clara Gissler went aboard the mailboat on 6 November 1905, never guessing that they were saying goodbye to Cocos Island for good. They got to Puntarenas on 8 November, intending to return to the island in a week's time. However, it so happened that on 11 November a letter arrived from Gissler's brother Hermann in Remscheid. He was gravely ill, he wrote, so he urgently requested August to come home and take over the running of the paper factory at Betzdorf until he recovered. 'I'll gladly come home to help,' August wrote home. 'On the other hand, I don't like leaving the island, even temporarily, because we still haven't completed certain work relating to the treasure. But of course, it's my duty to help Hermann; so the island must simply wait a while.'

Clara and August took the next steamer to New York via Panama and sailed on to Antwerp, reaching there on 27 December. Back home in Remscheid it turned out that Hermann's state of health had dramatically improved in the interim. 'Hermann is fairly alright [sic] again', August noted on 6 January 1906. If he harboured any suspicions that his brother's illness had been merely a pretext for summoning him home after 20 years, he kept them to himself. After trying to make himself useful in the leatherboard and paper factory for three or four months, he got itchy feet again.

August and Clara Gissler never returned to Cocos Island. They settled in New York, where they led a poverty-stricken existence with August's sisters Alma and Emmy, who earned a living as maidservants; Alma had emigrated to America as a young woman, Emmy had left Germany when her marriage broke up. To the last, Gissler believed himself to be a wealthy man. Even though he had failed to find the Lima Treasure, he considered himself the legal owner of Cocos Island. Although suffering from rheumatism and stomach trouble by the time Clara died in 1925, he persisted in hoping that someone would advance him enough money to enable him to recover the treasure. When he realized that this would never happen he tried to sell the island to the US Navy as a base, but that plan, too, came to nothing. He died on 8 August 1935, at the age of 78. His will decreed that his property on Cocos Island should be divided among 13 relatives, friends and financial backers. It further stipulated that, should the land be sold, it must not be disposed of for less than $200,000.* However, since the official estimate of its value was only $500, the heirs made representations to the Costa Rican government. They were informed that since August Gissler had neither found the treasure nor established a permanent settlement, he had never owned Cocos Island, only been granted its usufruct. There could thus be no question of his leaving it to them.

---

*Gissler's will, dated 5 February 1929, was published in the *New York Times* on 13 November 1935. It specified that his two New York sisters, Alma and Emmy, and two friends in New York and Ocean City should each receive three-twentieths of his estate on Cocos Island. His sisters Anna and Johanna back home in Remscheid were to get one-twentieth apiece, as were his nephew Walter Gissler, who had taken over the family firm; his uncle Richard Berger, a paper manufacturer of Wolkenburg (Saxony); and four other persons.

7

The Bottle Imp

THE SAMOANS took to the amiable Scot who was so unlike the starchy gentlemen from the Deutsche Handelsgesellschaft. They admired the big house that was taking shape at Vailima and the fabulous treasures he was accumulating there. He displayed more gaiety, generosity and charm than any other European in Samoa, and, since his clan was steadily increasing, he was locally regarded as a great and kindly chief. Although Louis, Fanny and Lloyd lived alone at Vailima for the first few months, they were soon joined by Fanny's daughter Belle and her son Austin, a little later by Belle's husband Joe Strong, and eventually by Louis's mother Margaret Stevenson and his cousin Graham Balfour.

In order to run Vailima, Louis employed 12 domestic servants and as many plantation workers, so 20 to 30 people lived on his money. Then there was the cost of clothing, food and medicines. Fanny's horticultural experiments also cost money, as did her perfume distillery, which never went into production, and her domestic animals, which were forever getting lost in the jungle. The little gilt rings that Belle gave the maidservants cost money. Lloyd's riding boots cost money. So did the horse on which he ordered the plantation workers around and the ice machine he brought with him from Scotland, which never worked properly. Joe Strong's addiction to drink and women cost money. The splendid house, which was always threatening to be swallowed up by jungle, cost money. And before long, when he went to school in California, little Austin would cost money too.

Louis met all these obligations with the sense of duty proper to a clan chieftain. He made sure that grace was said at table every day. He gave the children religious instruction and taught them history.

At Christmas, Easter and Whitsun he issued his Samoan household staff with kilts in the Stuart tartan and commanded them to wear these over their tattooed loins. And when a forced labourer fled to Vailima from the German plantation overseers' whips, he took him in and paid the Handelsgesellschaft an indemnity.

EARLY IN 1891 the London Missionary Society asked Louis for a contribution to the missionary weekly *O le Sulu o Samoa,* the first and only periodical in the Samoan language. He was to write the natives a morally uplifting tale, and the missionaries would translate it into Samoan. The story, which was entitled *The Bottle Imp,* appeared in instalments from May to December 1891. Read with intense interest by every literate Samoan, it remained Upolu's principal topic of conversation for many months. To the end of his days, Robert Louis Stevenson failed to dissuade the Samoans from identifying him with the hero of the story and, consequently, from regarding him with a mixture of awe and compassion, envy and abhorrence.[1]

The Samoans were unaware of the difference between fiction and fact. All that they had read so far was the Bible and its interpretation by the missionaries: every printed word was the word of God, whose truth it was impossible to doubt. So they read Louis's story, too, as they would have read another chapter from the Bible; in other words, as a statement of fact. Everyone instantly realized who was hidden behind the story's ill-disguised hero. No one in Apia was deceived by the fact that his name was Keawe, not Louis, and that the story took place in Hawaii, not Samoa. No one with eyes in his head could have failed to grasp the truth as soon as he read the description of the luckless hero's house, in which he had, as a youth, become fabulously wealthy in an unaccountably short space of time.

> Now the house stood on the mountainside, visible to ships. Above, the forest ran up into the clouds of rain; below, the black lava fell in cliffs, where the kings of old lay buried. A garden bloomed about that house with every hue of flowers; and there was an orchard of papaia [papaya] on the one hand and an orchard of breadfruit on the other, and right in front, toward the sea, a ship's mast had been rigged up and bore a flag. As for the house, it was three stories high, with great chambers and broad balconies on each. The windows were of glass, so excellent that it was as clear as water and as bright as day. All manner of furniture

adorned the chambers. Pictures hung upon the walls in golden frames: pictures of ships, and of men fighting, and of the most beautiful women, and of singular places; nowhere in the world are there pictures of so bright a colour as Keawe found hanging in his house. As for the knick-knacks, they were extraordinary fine; chiming clocks and musical boxes, little men with nodding heads, books filled with pictures, weapons of price from all quarters of the world, and the most elegant puzzles to entertain a solitary man. And as no one would care to live in such chambers, only to walk through and view them, the balconies were made so broad that a whole town might have lived on them in delight; and Keawe knew not which to prefer, whether the back porch, where you got the land breeze, and looked upon the orchards and the flowers, or the front balcony, where you could drink the wind of the sea ...[2]

In spite of his magnificent house, Keawe could never feel truly happy because he had acquired his wealth by means of a pact with the Devil. Not so long ago he had been a poor but honest fellow who 'could read and write like a schoolmaster', and who had spent a long time voyaging around the Pacific Ocean as a sailor. But one day ...

... it came in Keawe's mind to have a sight of the great world and foreign cities, and he shipped on a vessel bound to San Francisco. This is a fine town, with a fine harbour, and rich people uncountable; and, in particular, there is one hill which is covered with palaces. Upon this hill Keawe was one day taking a walk with his pocket full of money, viewing the great houses upon either hand with pleasure. 'What fine houses these are!' he was thinking, 'and how happy must those people be who dwell in them, and take no care for the morrow!' The thought was in his mind when he came abreast of a house that was smaller than some others, but all finished and beautified like a toy; the steps of that house shone like silver, and the borders of the garden bloomed like garlands, and the windows were bright like diamonds; and Keawe stopped and wondered at the excellence of all he saw. So stopping, he was aware of a man that looked forth upon him through a window so clear that Keawe could see him as you see a fish in a pool upon the reef. The man was elderly, with a bald head and a black beard; and his face was heavy with sorrow, and he bitterly sighed. And the truth of it is, that as Keawe looked in on the man, and the man looked out upon Keawe, each envied the other.[3]

In fact, the old man owed his wealth to an imp who was imprisoned in a little bottle and brought its owner any conceivable thing for which he asked – love, fame, victory in battle, all the riches in the world – with the exception of good health and a longer life. The trouble was, anyone in possession of the bottle at the hour of his death was inescapably doomed to go to hell. He could get rid of the bottle only by selling it more cheaply – for ready cash – than he had bought it. Many centuries ago the Devil had introduced it into the world at an immense price. Since then it had passed through human history, becoming cheaper and cheaper every time it changed hands. Napoleon Bonaparte had owned the bottle and risen to become 'king of the world' before selling it on and being overthrown. Thanks to the bottle, Captain James Cook had discovered countless islands in the Pacific before selling it and being 'slain upon Hawaii'. And now, here was this old man in San Francisco who, having originally paid $90 for the bottle, had spent many years looking for someone who would take it off his hands for a lower price. 'All you have to do,' he told Keawe, 'is use the power of the imp in moderation, and then sell it to someone else, as I do to you, and finish your life in comfort.'

In Stevenson's story Keawe clinches the deal but is then beset by misfortune: he cannot find a taker for the bottle. To the Samoans it was immediately and blindingly obvious that Keawe could be none other than Robert Louis Stevenson. Wasn't he fabulously wealthy? Wasn't he, like Keawe, a cheerful person who couldn't help singing for joy at the top of his voice as he walked round his beautiful house? Wasn't he, on the other hand, chronically ill – a condition for which the Bottle Imp could do nothing? Wasn't he suddenly overcome with sadness when he thought no one was looking? And what of his wife Fanny? The Samoans called her Aolele, or Flying Cloud, because her face, too, although wreathed in smiles a moment before, could abruptly cloud over. The maids had often seen her shed surreptitious and inexplicable tears. The Samoans decided that the story of Keawe provided an explanation for all these things. The Bottle Imp must be hidden somewhere in Vailima. If that were so, Louis must get rid of the bottle as soon as possible in order to preserve his soul from hell. Could it be that he would never find a buyer? Had he been foolish enough to buy the bottle for only 1 cent, the lowest price possible, with the result that, even if he found a buyer, the latter would be unable to undercut him? Could it be that his soul was irrevocably doomed?

To the end of his days, Robert Louis Stevenson strove in vain to make his Samoan visitors grasp the difference between fiction and fact. 'Parties who come up to visit my unpretentious mansion, after having admired the ceilings by Vanderputty and the tapestry by Gob-bling, manifest towards the end a certain uneasiness which proves them to be fellows of an infinite delicacy. They may be seen to shrug a brown shoulder, to roll up a speaking eye, and at last the secret bursts from them: "Where is the bottle?"'[4]

8

Where *is* the Treasure?

I T IS TRULY SURPRISING that, in 150 years, not a single treasure map, satellite picture or metal detector has pinpointed the treasure's actual location on Cocos Island, and that it has not been discovered by methodical German diligence, brilliant Gallic adventurism, or even the brute force exerted by American dynamite and bulldozers. In fact, we know perfectly well where the Lima Treasure must be buried. As far as we can judge, the *Mary Dear* can only have dropped anchor off the island's north-west coast, in Chatham or Wafer Bay, the only safe anchorages for a large vessel capable of carrying many tons of cargo. Thompson's men would have had no choice but to row the treasure chests ashore in dinghies and land them on one of those two beaches. Nor, after unloading them, could they have transported such heavy loads far into the interior. The beaches are only ten or twenty yards deep, and it would have been an immensely strenuous job to haul treasure chests weighing several hundredweight up the steep, jungle-clad slopes immediately beyond them. In order to conceal them in the interior of the island, Thompson's men would have had to cut a path through the undergrowth at least 6 feet wide. They would then have had to make several dozen trips along this path, back and forth, back and forth, creating a beaten track on which no grass would grow for months. Although this would have blazed a trail to the treasure's hiding-place, the Spanish soldiers who searched the two bays some weeks later, accompanied by Thompson and his mate, could detect no damage to the jungle vegetation. For these reasons, and because the cache had to be easily and quickly accessible, common sense dictates that the only places that enter into consideration are the beaches themselves, or possibly the bed of a small river flowing from the interior, but the latter very soon traverses steep rocks and deep basins.

Until now, almost all treasure-hunters have concentrated on those two strips of beach in Chatham and Wafer Bay, which between them cover an area of two or three football pitches. During the twentieth century, many treasure-hunters extended their search to the few hundred square yards of stony seabed exposed at low tide. All the areas with sandy subsoil – on the beaches and in the water – must be ruled out, however, because gold would have sunk beyond recovery on account of its high specific gravity. All in all, then, what remains is a readily surveyable area which has been repeatedly dug up, ploughed up, blown up and sieved – invariably without success. This being so, the time has now come to ask a crucial question: Did Captain Thompson bury the Lima Treasure on Cocos Island at all? Isn't it far more likely that he sailed to another island?

There is a popular and romantic notion that pirates who had won a sea battle and plundered their victims used to hurry off in search of some remote, godforsaken island on which to bury their loot on the beach, hide it in a cave, or submerge it just offshore. This was seldom so in reality. In the first place, their loot tended to consist of coffee or silk, sugar or tobacco, hardly ever of weatherproof and waterproof gold coins and precious stones. Perishable goods, which did not lend themselves to burying or submerging, had to be taken to the nearest port and converted into cash as quickly as possible. Even when their loot really did consist of precious metal, pirates seldom chose to go to the trouble of burying it somewhere with a view to retrieving it in the far distant future. They lived from day to day, giving no thought to a future in which they anyway expected little more than a bullet in the head, a knife in the guts or a noose round the neck. As a rule, they divided up their haul immediately after a raid and made for a port whose authorities didn't ask too many questions, where they drank, whored and gambled away their ill-gotten gains in readiness for their next raid. Only a few pirate captains such as Henry Every and Henry Morgan were shrewd enough to fulfil their get-rich-quick ambitions, buy off the law and lead prosperous, respectable lives in retirement.

THERE HAS ALWAYS, ever since the days of Thompson and Keating, been a handful of men who believed they were the only people in the world to know the exact location of the treasure on Cocos Island:

behind a rock in a man-made cave; in a natural cave visible only at low tide; beneath the roots of some palm tree or other; or so-many paces in this or that direction from this or that rock. They usually possessed hand-drawn maps of very old, unique and authentic appearance, but few of them ever asked themselves why on earth Thompson, Davis or Bonito would have bothered to draw maps when they had buried the treasure themselves, knew its location perfectly well, intended to retrieve it as soon as possible, and couldn't possibly have wanted anyone else to do that on their behalf.

It is also a striking fact that most treasure-hunters never lost faith, even when their hopes had been dashed again and again. They always blamed their failure on a wide variety of adverse circumstances: many were too poor, too ill or too rich to undertake the voyage; others made it to Cocos Island, but in foul weather, inadequately equipped or with unreliable associates. Still others had insufficient time at their disposal, were balked by the Costa Rican authorities, or found that invaluable landmarks had been destroyed by previous treasure-seekers. Every conceivable reason for failure was cited bar one: that the treasure simply wasn't there.

IT IS, OF COURSE, SAFE to assume that Thompson really did bury the treasure. For one thing, it consisted of thoroughly durable materials; for another, he could be certain that the whole of the Spanish navy would soon be hot on his heels; and, thirdly, all the *Mary Dear*'s seamen and officers swore under duress that they had buried the treasure on an island named Cocos Island – a statement to be taken all the more seriously because the 15 men were bound to be hanged and had little reason to agree to tell a concerted lie.

After more than 180 years of futile searching, however, it may be time to consider another possibility. What if the *Mary Dear* did *not* drop anchor in Chatham or Wafer Bay? If so, in what direction could she have fled in August 1821? Certainly not north or south, because no port on the west coast of North, Central or South America would have provided her with a bolt-hole. Not eastwards to the Atlantic either, because a light vessel like the *Mary Dear* would not have withstood the stormy voyage round Cape Horn. Her only remaining escape route led westwards and out into the Pacific Ocean, where Cocos Island would indeed have been the first possibility to present itself. However, it may have occurred to an experienced and circumspect captain like Thompson that the Spanish navy would hit on such an obvious hiding-place, and that it might be wiser to harness the strong Pacific current and sail much further to the west. In order to put as much distance as possible between himself and his pursuers, therefore, he would have crowded on sail and taken his ship as fast and as far away as he could from Lima, Peru and South America.

On this assumption, we can envisage the following scenario. The *Mary Dear* cruised westwards against the wind, as instructed, until she disappeared below the horizon. She then allowed the cold Humboldt Current to carry her north-west along the coast of South America and past the Galapagos Islands, where Captain Thompson may have taken on a few dozen turtles as a source of fresh meat. South of Cocos Island the Humboldt Current flows westwards into the warm Equatorial Current, on which the *Mary Dear* would probably have made good progress aided by the powerful trade winds. The storms associated with the rainy season were still far off in August, so it is quite possible that she reached the Polynesian archipelago quickly. Assuming that the good weather held, the pirates could have sailed past the Marquesas within a few weeks and ridden the Equatorial Current south-west for a few more days, passing Tahiti and the Society and Cook Islands. Thereafter, if she allowed her voyage to take its natural course, she would have headed straight for the islands of Samoa and Tonga.

That a rapid crossing of the Pacific was feasible had been demonstrated 15 years earlier by the British privateer *Port au Prince,* which had rendered the west coast of Spanish America unsafe for two years and was compelled to escape from the Spanish galleons bearing down on her. On 29 November 1806 she was anchored off the island of Lifuka in the Kingdom of Tonga. Two days later the *Port au Prince* was seized by hostile islanders. They slaughtered the pirates and stole their looted gold, then beached the vessel and set it ablaze in order to recover its valuable iron components. Tongan smiths would have used these to forge knives, spear points and battleaxes which may well exist to this day, but the gold disappeared.[1]

If more proof were required that the fastest escape route from Peru leads straight to the Polynesian archipelago, this was provided 141 years later by the Norwegian ethnologist Thor Heyerdahl. On 28 April 1947, in order to confirm his theory that the South Sea islands were colonized by settlers from South America, he set off on his balsa-wood raft *Kon-Tiki* from Callao, the very port where the *Mary Dear* took on the Lima Treasure. After drifting north-west past the Galapagos Islands on the Humboldt Current, *Kon-Tiki* was picked up by the South Equatorial Current and conveyed across 4,320 nautical miles of open sea to the Raroia Reef off Tahiti, where it was dashed to pieces on 7 August 1947, its 101st day at sea.

From a purely technical aspect, therefore, there is some evidence to suggest that Captain Thompson unloaded the Lima Treasure on a remote sandy beach that did *not* form part of Cocos Island but lay 6–7,000 nautical miles west of Chatham Bay – in other words, in the vicinity of the patch of jungle which Robert Louis Stevenson was to purchase 68 years later. On which of the innumerable South Sea islands this happened it is hard to say. All we know for sure is that Thompson and his crew referred to their treasure island, too, as Cocos Island. It is to be assumed that they ferried the heavy chests ashore in dinghies, dragged them across the beach and buried them further inland, where the subsoil was firmer. We may further assume that, once they had completed their work, they weighed anchor as quickly as possible, hoping to sail off into the blue unobserved and return at some future date, when the Spaniards had stopped looking for them.

Thompson had no alternative, because the formerly blank and uncharted expanses on maps in which an outlawed ship could hide from the long arm of authority had long since ceased to exist.* Nowhere in the world was there a reasonably navigable harbour that was not closely watched by a British and a French consul, as well as by official representatives of the Netherlands, Spain, Portugal and the United States. Lloyd's insurance agents, who were stationed everywhere, reported all shipping movements to London and noted everything worth knowing about vessels' ports of origin and destinations, cargoes and crews. Thus the men of the *Mary Dear* had only one course open to them: a return to legality. In other words, they would

---

*The mutineers from HMS *Bounty* had learnt this to their cost 32 years earlier, after they cast their captain, William Bligh, adrift in a 23-foot launch on 28 April 1789 – quite close to the Tongan island of Tofua. Most of the mutineers were arrested in Tahiti two years later and shipped back to England in irons. Only nine succeeded in escaping to Pitcairn, probably the most remote of all South Sea islands, whose exact position was then still unknown. The isolated mutineers soon fell out and within a few years most had been killed, but their descendants continue to live on Pitcairn Island to this day.

have to sail back to Spanish America and rehabilitate themselves in the eyes of the law by means of as plausible a lie as they could devise.

This they did. Thompson, who was an experienced sea captain, would have sailed north for some days until the *Mary Dear* had crossed the equator. Immediately to the north of it, the equatorial counter-current flows steadily eastwards, all year round, at a speed of 2 knots. A ship that abandons herself to it can rely on making a landfall in Central America on a level with Costa Rica. And that, as history records, is precisely where Captain Thompson and his men were picked up by a Spanish frigate, clapped in irons and taken for questioning.

9

The Adventurous Voyage of Willem Schouten and Jacob Le Maire

I F CAPTAIN THOMPSON did not, therefore, hide the Lima Treasure off Costa Rica but on some South Sea island much further west, where exactly did he go? In order to reconstruct the voyage of the *Mary Dear* it is helpful to study the logbooks of the earliest Christian seafarers in the Pacific.

Two hundred years before the *Mary Dear*, a ship ventured to leave the coast of South America, sail out into the Pacific with the aid of the Equatorial Current and follow the setting sun for days and weeks on end. This was the Dutch three-masted barque *Eendracht* under the command of Jacob Le Maire, which in 1616 was the very first ship to round Cape Horn, cross the Pacific and, in the process, make an interesting discovery.

Jacob Le Maire was the first-born son of Isaac Le Maire, one of the wealthiest citizens in Hoorn, a seaport not far from Amsterdam. In June 1615 his father had sent him off with two ships, the *Eendracht* and the *Hoorn*, to find a new trade route to the East Indies. He was not to sail eastwards by the usual route round Africa and across the Indian Ocean, but westwards across the Atlantic. Then, after rounding the southernmost tip of South America, he was to explore the still unknown Pacific Ocean.

Old Isaac Le Maire had made his fortune by investing in trade with China, the East Indies and the Caribbean. He had been one of the backers of a venture in 1595, when Dutch merchants sailed to Indonesia to break the Portuguese monopoly of the spice trade. His money had also been involved, in 1597, when four East India companies were founded in various Dutch towns. In the ensuing five years they dispatched no less than 65 ships to Sumatra, Java, Borneo and the Philippines and drove the Portuguese out of the market. When the four East India companies waged a ruinous price war among themselves, Isaac Le Maire was one of the first to grasp a basic principle of the free market economy: that competition between businesses may be commercially stimulating, but it also reduces profit margins. On 20 March 1602, in order to maximize the selling prices of pepper, cinnamon, nutmeg and cloves and purchase them as cheaply as possible, the four companies combined to form a single trading house, the United East India Company (Vereenigde Oost-Indische Compagnie, VOC). It had two novel features. One was that not only wealthy merchant princes put money into it; craftsmen, employees and domestic servants could also invest. Secondly, share capital was invested for the long term, not just for a single voyage. Thus the VOC was the first modern joint stock company in the world. From then on, the company claimed exclusive rights over trade between the Netherlands and the East Indies. No other Dutch ship was permitted to sail to the East Indies round the Cape of Good Hope or through the Strait of Magellan. Anyone who violated this ban incurred a heavy fine and imprisonment.

The VOC quickly became the world's biggest commercial concern. In the following 200 years it waged unimaginably brutal wars of conquest and built forts and castles and supply depots along its shipping routes. The 1,600 vessels built in the company's own shipyards undertook a total of 6,000 voyages. The vast majority returned home laden with Javanese pepper, Chinese porcelain, elephants from Ceylon and cotton from the Coromandel Coast. Only 120 voyages, or 2 per cent, ended in the loss of a ship.

From the outset, the company's biggest shareholder and most influential director was Isaac Le Maire. The 97,000 guilders he had invested in it yielded fabulous dividends. Only a year after the VOC was founded, however, he grasped another law of the free market economy: that although being tied to a monopoly guarantees big profit margins for minimal risks, it restricts the initiative of any freedom-loving entrepreneur. Accordingly, behind the back of the company whose principal shareholder he was, Isaac Le Maire fitted out a fleet of 14 ships for a voyage to the East Indies that would circumvent the monopoly and avoid paying dues. All the vessels returned safely and their cargoes were sold for a huge profit, but the truth came out. Fearing for their monopoly, the company's share-holders accused Le Maire of fraud and a conflict of interests, and he was eventually compelled to retire from the VOC board in disgrace.

From that day on, Le Maire made it his life's ambition to break the East India Company's monopoly by opening up a new sea route to the East Indies. If the south-east routes were forbidden him, he would sail to Asia across the unexplored Arctic Ocean, making his way along the Norwegian coast to the North Cape and then between the North Pole and Siberia to Japan and, eventually, China. Although it was known that all kinds of dangers lay in wait for Christian seafarers in the Arctic, opening up the North-East Passage would almost halve the sailing distance between Europe and the East Indies.

Unable to find a partner in the Netherlands, Isaac Le Maire turned to Catholic France – a bold step for a Calvinist businessman to take in times of religious strife. However, the throne of France was then occupied by Henry IV, a Protestant by birth who had adopted Catholicism for form's sake only. The king evinced great interest in founding a French East India Company, and he and Le Maire agreed to send out an expeditionary ship commanded by a Dutch captain under the Dutch colours. If a new route really was found, the vessel would hoist the Bourbon flag and sail straight back to France, and the route would be named after the king.

The expedition set off on 5 May 1609 and headed north. Passing Norway, Finland and Spitzbergen, it turned into the Barents Sea a long way north of the Arctic Circle, but the French colours were never hoisted. After three months the polar winter set in, the sea froze, and the ship had to turn back. Henry IV's assassination by a Catholic fanatic soon afterwards put paid to Le Maire's collaboration with France.

But he clung to his aim of breaking the VOC's monopoly. If the North-East Passage was impracticable, he would try going in the opposite direction, or south-west. The monopoly expressly included the Strait of Magellan, which lay between the South American mainland and the islands of Tierra del Fuego, but if Le Maire's ship left the Strait of Magellan to starboard, proceeded even further south to the southernmost tip of Tierra del Fuego and then turned west into the Pacific, that would be a new and hitherto unused shipping route and the letter of the law would be observed. In the greatest secrecy, Le Maire got together with Willem Schouten, an experienced Hoorn merchant and sea captain, and fitted out two ships which sailed from the Netherlands on 14 June 1615. The *Eendracht,* a barque of 220 tons, was commanded by Willem Schouten himself; the *Hoorn,* which was half her size, by Le Maire's son Jacob. The purpose of the voyage was kept a close secret; not even the crews were informed until four months later, when the Brazilian coast was in sight. On 8 December the expedition entered Puerto Deseado, where both ships were to be overhauled and provisioned for the hardest part of the voyage around the southern tip of South America, but the *Hoorn* caught fire while sea-grass was being burnt off and sank in the harbour basin, sending up a great cloud of smoke and steam. The crew just had time to transfer her eight cannon, the anchor and themselves to the *Eendracht.* Heavily laden and with a double crew, the remaining ship continued on her way. The *Eendracht* sailed past the Strait of Magellan according to plan, and on 25 January 1616 a favourable current carried her into the strait south of Tierra del Fuego, as Schouten had hoped. On 29 January the *Eendracht* at last reached the southernmost point of her voyage, a cape which Schouten named 'Kap Hoorn' in honour of his home town. For a whole month the ship sailed north along the Chilean coast in heavy seas, but at the end of February the *Eendracht* encountered the favourable winds and currents that would, in centuries to come, carry the *Port au Prince,* the *Mary Dear* and *Kon-Tiki* westwards across the Pacific. Willem Schouten and Jacob Le Maire conscientiously kept a daily log and charted their voyage.

The first South Sea islands hove in sight a good month later. The exhausted men went ashore as often as they could to take on fruit and meat and replace the stale water in their barrels with fresh. They soon made the acquaintance of the islanders.

> These people were completely naked, women and men alike, with only a scrap of cloth covering their private parts. Their complexion was reddish, and they had rubbed themselves with some kind of oil or fat; the women had cut their hair short, but the men wore theirs very long and dyed black. Their boat was a wonderful construction of strange design; it consisted of two long, handsome canoes which lay side by side in the water a considerable distance apart and were joined in the middle by two wide planks of wood. They were very good seamen, having no compass or other instruments with them, only fish hooks made of stone and turtles' bones.

On 10 May 1616 a small, conical volcanic island appeared on the horizon, and two or three cannon shots away from it a smaller, flatter island. Willem Schouten described it as:

> very high and blue, and only some eight leagues distant; but, although we had a favourable wind, we could not get any nearer all day, so we kept watch during the night so as to be able to put in the next day. That evening we sighted a sail, and shortly afterwards another quite some distance from the coast. We supposed them to be fishing boats, because they kept sailing back and forth. At night they lit a fire and drew near to one another. The following morning we approached the island, which was very high. Then one of the sailing boats came towards us and we let down a bucket over the stern. Since the men could not reach it, one of them dived overboard and seized it. They then untied the bucket from the rope, and, in its place, attached two coconuts and three or four flying fish; and then they very loudly shouted something we could not understand, but we took it they meant us to haul in the rope again. We had scarcely dropped anchor when another three boats approached and circled us, together with nine or ten canoes, two of which had hoisted a small white flag as a sign of peace, whereupon we did the same. There were three or four men seated in each canoe. The canoes, which had blunt bows and sharp sterns, were made entirely from a single piece of redwood and were remarkably fast. When they were close enough to our ship, the men dived overboard and swam across with their hands filled with coconuts and yam roots, which they wanted to exchange for nails and glass beads. They were so enamoured of these that they exchanged four or five coconuts for a single nail or a few glass beads. Thus we exchanged 180 coconuts that day. So many people crowded on board that we did not know what to do. And, when we sent our rowing boat over to the other island to look for a better anchorage less exposed to the open sea, it was at once surrounded by twelve or thirteen canoes from the other island. But their occupants, who seemed to be very angry, had sticks of hardwood with them, the ends of which were blackened and sharpened. They climbed into our boat and tried to steal it, so our men had to defend themselves and fired three musket shots. The islanders did not at first take this seriously, but laughed and jeered at our men, doubtless believing the muskets to be only playthings. But when the third ball penetrated the chest of one of their number with such force that it emerged from his back, they hurried to his aid and summoned the other boats.

On the morning of 12 May it rained. This time the *Eendracht* was approached by a fleet of 35 canoes, all heavily laden with coconuts and other fruit. She was soon so thronged with canoes that their occupants bundled up their wares, jumped overboard and dived beneath their competitors in order to reach the ship. So many of them clambered up the side that the sailors had to beat them off with cudgels. Any islander that did manage to reach the deck and complete a transaction dived overboard and swam back to his canoe.

On the morning of 13 May, however, at least one hundred and forty-five canoes came to trade with us, additionally accompanied by a fleet of twenty-three sailing boats. Five or six men were seated in each canoe and twenty-five in each sailing boat; what their intentions were, we did not know. We were soon exchanging nails for coconuts, and all behaved as if we were the best of friends. We soon discovered, however, that the opposite was true. Not for the first time, they invited us over to the other island. After breakfast we weighed anchor to go there. Then the king approached us in a sailing boat and called to us very loudly. We would gladly have welcomed him aboard, but he refused, which we took to be a bad omen, and the more so when all the canoes and sailing boats gathered ever closer around us. Before long, a drum was beaten aboard the king's sailing boat. Then they all raised a very loud cry, which we construed as the signal to attack our ship.

The king's boat carried a sail adorned with a grey and red cockerel. Having lined up behind it in battle order, all the sailing boats and canoes attacked with a furious roar. The islanders were armed with stones, the Dutch with muskets. Two or three volleys left several dead and wounded floating in the water and the attackers fled in panic.

We continued our voyage in a west-south-westerly direction because we assumed that the king, who had over a thousand men at his disposal, one of whom, incidentally, was white, would soon have regrouped his forces. After we had gone about four leagues, many of our men expressed a wish to return to the island and land there by force in order to replenish our meagre supply of water. But the commanders of the ship forbade this.[1]

Instead, Willem Schouten and Jacob Le Maire retired to the chart room to enter up their log and map. They christened the flat, elongated island 'Verrader Eylandt' (Traitors' Island) because most of the attackers had come from there, but the higher, volcanic island, probably because it was densely wooded with coconut palms, they named Cocos Eylandt.

Schouten's and Le Maire's chart gives its position as 16° 10' south. This is a remarkably accurate computation. Modern, satellite-based navigational instruments locate the island at 15.85° south and 173.71° west. That the Dutchmen did not give its latitude should not be held against them; the requisite technical aids were not available until the 18th century.

So there is a second, forgotten Cocos Island situated 1,243 miles south and 4,970 miles west of the Cocos Island off the coast of Central America to which so many references have been made above. Above all, though, it is only 166 miles from Samoa; on a clear day, its volcanic peak is visible from the hills of Upolu. Cocos Eylandt retained its Dutch name on many 17th- and 18th-century marine charts. It was not until the beginning of the 19th century that the name became obsolete and was replaced by the Polynesian designation 'Tafahi'.*

---

*Many publications retained the Dutch name until Robert Louis Stevenson's time. In 1879 the *Nouveau Dictionnaire de Géographie Universelle* stated that there were many Cocos Islands in the Indian and Pacific Oceans. Among those mentioned were one in the Bay of Bengal (Keeling Islands), a group of islands north-east of Papua New Guinea, Tafahi, and the Cocos Island off the coast of Central America.

10

Is There a Screw Loose?

THE UNPREJUDICED OBSERVER cannot fail to notice that the two Cocos Islands bear an almost uncanny resemblance. Both display the conical shape typical of extinct volcanoes, they are similar in height and area and are densely overgrown with coconut palms. Discounting their geographical position, what mainly distinguishes them is that the one off Costa Rica is the most internationally celebrated of all treasure islands, whereas the one south of Samoa has never officially been visited by treasure-hunters.

Robert Louis Stevenson never said a word about his having settled more or less within sight of another Cocos Island in December 1889. No reference to a Cocos Island can be found anywhere in his literary estate. Letters, poems, short stories, South Seas novels – none of them alludes to either island, not even by the Polynesian name Tafahi. It seems positively suspicious that he makes no mention of Samoa's southern neighbour, given that no island in the South Seas was too remote and insignificant for him to visit it, and that his letters, articles and novels always contained references to his travels. He was forever on the move from one island to another throughout his five years in the Pacific. He undertook shortish trips by starlight with his friends William Clarke, the missionary, and Harold Sewall, the US consul. He also went on longer voyages by mailboat to Hawaii in the north and Australia and New Zealand in the south, so he must have passed Tafahi on several occasions. Graham Balfour, his cousin and official biographer, pointed out that, before his time in Samoa, Louis

> had spent an almost equal length of time in visiting other islands in the Pacific. In fact, had he been deliberately preparing himself for the life he

was to lead, he could hardly have pursued a wiser course, or undergone a more thorough training. On his travels he enjoyed exceptional opportunities of gathering information, and in general knowledge of the South Seas, and of Samoa in particular, he was probably at the time of his death rivalled by no more than two or three persons of anything like his education or intelligence.[1]

There was scarcely a single group of islands within a wide radius of Samoa on which Louis had not set foot. Sheer curiosity prompted him to visit the Gilbert and Ellice Islands; the Marshall Islands; New Caledonia; Olosenga; Pukopuka; Nassau Island; Penrhyn Island, where leprosy was raging; and Suwarrow, long rumoured to be the site of buried pirate treasure. But Tafahi – which was, so to speak, on his doorstep – merits not a word in any of his extant writings.

In view of all this, one is tempted to pose the question yet again: What reasons could he have had for deciding, seemingly on the spur of the moment, to spend the rest of his days in Samoa, that most inconspicuous of South Seas beauties? Surprisingly enough, it is a question to which little attention has been devoted by any of the 150-odd biographers who have recounted his life story in the past 100 years. Without exception, they consider it an established fact, and unworthy of further explanation, that he remained in Samoa primarily for his health's sake. The author himself never tires of mentioning in his letters how robust he has become; that he spends hours in the saddle, swims in the ocean and roams the mountains for days on end. This bragging was not only uncharacteristic of him but at odds with the truth; his victory fanfares were undoubtedly intended to reassure worried friends and relations back in Britain. It is apparent from many incidental remarks – often designed to excuse him for not writing sooner – that his bouts of fever were quite as frequent as they had been in California or the south of France; that he coughed up blood every few months, just as he had in Davos or Edinburgh; and that in Samoa, as anywhere else in the world, every cold brought him to death's door.

5 December 1889: 'Everything going splendidly but health; so long a time on a low island diet is indeed something of a trial.'

7 March 1890: 'This visit to Sydney has smashed me handsomely.'

13 July 1890: 'To my unaffected annoyance the blood-spitting racket has started again.'

August 1890: 'I have the cough-mill to go through at night, and do not love it.'

August 1890: '[I am] at my old trade – bed-ridden.'

November 1890: 'I have a fever at present.'

January 1891: 'I ought to see an oculist, being very blind indeed – and sometimes unable to read.'

February 1891: 'Have had a swingeing sharp attack in Sydney.'

March 1891: 'I am just (and scarce) afoot again after a smoking hot little malady at Sydney.'

April 1891: 'The other day I was three-and-twenty hours in an open boat; it has made me pretty ill; but fancy it's not killing me half-way!'

June 1891: 'I have a touch of fever again.'

January 1892: 'I have been down all month with influenza and am only just recovering [...] for three weeks I have not touched a pen with my finger.'

March 1892: 'I am now an old, but healthy skeleton.'

May 1892: 'I was sharply ill on Wednesday. [...] I am a wreck, as no doubt style and handwriting both testify. [...] If only I could secure a violent death, what a fine success! I wish to die in my boots; no more land of counterpane for me. To be drowned, to be shot, to be thrown from a horse – aye, to be hanged, rather than pass again through that slow dissolution.'

August 1892: '... "belly belong me" has been kicking up, and I have just taken 15 drops of laudanum.'

30 September 1892: '*David Balfour* done, and its author along with it, or nearly.'

28 October 1892: 'I have had a very annoying fever with symptoms of sore arm.'

7 April 1893: 'I am broken on the wheel, or feel like it.'

2 June 1893: 'I am nearly dead with dyspepsia, over-smoking, and unremunerative overwork.'

18 June 1893: 'I have had to stop all drink except some brandy in my coffee after dinner, and occasionally some brandy at night. Smoking I am trying to stop also; my health being hopelessly shattered by both these indulgencies.'

August 1893: 'I have had to lay aside my tennis, having (as was to be expected) had a smart but eminently brief haemorrhage.'

7 December 1893: 'I have been much prevented [from writing] of late, having carried out thoroughly to my own satisfaction two considerable illnesses.'

April 1894: 'I am daily better in physical health. [...] I was meant to die
    young, and the Gods do not love me.'
June 1894: 'I have had a vile cold which has prostrated me for more than
    a fortnight, and even now tears me nightly with spasmodic coughs.'
October 1894: 'As for me, there is nothing the matter with me in the
    world, beyond the disgusting circumstance that I am not so young
    as once I was.'
1 December 1894, three days before his death: 'I have in fact lost the
    path that makes it easy and natural for you to descend the hill. I am
    going at it straight. And where I have to go down it is a precipice.'[2]

No, Robert Louis Stevenson was not a well man in Samoa. That
the legend of his recovery should have persisted so stubbornly, despite
all the evidence to the contrary, is very odd. It is simply untrue that
he benefited from the climate in Samoa, where whole districts were
depopulated by dengue fever, elephantiasis and virulent influenza
and measles epidemics. What is true is that he was confined to bed
every few weeks. It is also true that the price he paid for every little
game of tennis on the court at Vailima was a haemorrhage. Last but
not least, it is a fact that on the day he set foot in Samoa he had less
than five years to live. In Scotland he might well have survived longer.

John Davis, a picture postcard photographer from Apia, took
some family photographs on the veranda at Vailima in May 1892.
These also tell a story that differs from the officially accepted version.
They show a mature man courageously holding himself erect and
gazing at the camera with the dignified air of a Scottish chieftain, but
certainly not a young Lochinvar whose iron constitution enables him
to spend hours swimming in the sea. His imminent demise is written
on his face, his bony frame gaunter and his hair sparser than ever,
and the eyes above his cheek-bones are ominously dark-ringed. It may
have accorded with his boyish love of adventure to visit remote volcanic islands aboard small sailing boats, just as it may have revived his
spirits to play the patriarch in his jungle residence. But that his health
improved so greatly in Samoa that it would have been irrational for
him to live anywhere else was a myth which he himself – perhaps
with good reason – carefully cultivated. He contradicted himself
only once when granting an interview to the *Christchurch Press* of
New Zealand. If his reasons for living in Samoa were solely medical,
he said, he would sooner go to hell. Honolulu would have done him
just as much good, and the Alps would probably have been still better

for him. If he had chosen Samoa instead of Honolulu, it was for the simple and extremely satisfying reason that it was less civilized. [3]

If his reasons for settling in Samoa were not medical, could they have been psychological? Were the Stevensons so happy in their jungle paradise that they couldn't conceive of returning to civilization? Anyone reading the official memoirs of members of the family would tend to believe so. Louis's letters almost always depict family life at Vailima in the rosiest of hues; Fanny's diary describes those years as the blissful, uninterrupted Robinsonade of a family whose members were bound together by ties of unclouded love. Her daughter Belle paints daily life in Samoa in the most delicate pastel shades, and Lloyd Osbourne's memoirs endorse this: 'Stevenson may not have been always happy in Vailima, but of one thing I am sure; he was happier there than he could have been in any other place in the world.' [4]

Once again, the group photographs mentioned above tell quite a different story. This is no happy family assembled on the steps of the veranda at Vailima. There isn't a single photograph in which they manage, if only for a few seconds' exposure time, to convey a semblance of harmony. On the contrary, each picture portrays a family whose members are trapped in a spider's web of mutual pretensions, antipathies and dependences. The focus of the scene is always Louis, the dignified patriarch. On his right sits his mother, a ramrod-backed figure in a snow-white widow's bonnet; on his left Fanny, a volcano of violent emotions capable of erupting at any moment. Standing on the top step is Lloyd, a young dandy wearing a white hat, riding boots and an immaculate white tropical suit, who misses the excitements of Paris, London and San Francisco in this lonely, insular environment. Seated one step lower is Belle with her son Austin on her lap. Puffy-eyed, she is leaning towards Lafaele, her muscular, handsome Samoan manservant, who sits protectively beside her with his knee pressed against hers, staring boldly at the camera. On the other side of the picture, a long way from Belle and the rest of the family, stands Joe Strong, her unfaithful drunk of a husband. He's lounging against a post with a white kakadu on his shoulder – Cocky by name, its linguistic talents were limited to the words 'Mamma, Mamma' – and is gazing darkly across at his wife and child, who are sitting as far away from him as possible.

No, they certainly weren't happy at Vailima. All of them were imprisoned on their little island amid the Pacific Ocean's boundless watery wastes, thousands of miles from the cafés and boulevards and drawing-rooms of home, from the galleries and newspaper offices and publishing houses and theatres where they could have pursued the respective artistic ambitions nursed by every member of the family save Margaret Stevenson. Fanny wanted to paint and write, Belle wanted to draw and dance, Joe Strong wanted to paint, Lloyd wanted to write novels, and even ten-year-old Austin was already looking for a publisher for his poems. Sadly, however, Fanny's oil paints melted in the tropical heat; the jungle could not provide Belle with an audience that might have appreciated her talent for drawing and dancing; Lloyd probably guessed that he would never, as a writer, emerge from Louis's shadow; and young Austin realized to his chagrin that he needed a little more practice. As for Joe Strong, his addiction to drink and women simply left him no time to devote to the fine arts. It was inevitable, therefore, that the only successful member of the family should have been regarded with unspoken envy – a sentiment that became all the more bitter the more his reputation grew. That everyone at Vailima subsisted mainly on Louis's income was a further humiliation which Fanny resented more than most.

> I wish I were able to write a little tale that I might save some money of my own ... I wonder what would become of a man, and to what he would degenerate, if his life was that of a woman's [sic]: to get 'the run of her teeth' [her dentist's bills paid] and presents of her clothes, and supposed to be always under bonds of the deepest gratitude for any further sums. I would work very hard to earn a couple of pounds a month, and I could easily earn much more, but there is my position as Louis's wife, therefore I cannot.'[5]

Conversely, Louis made demands on his family. From his wife he expected daily solicitude, from his mother unconditional admiration, and from his stepdaughter a readiness to take dictation whenever he suffered from writer's cramp. Little Austin, too, was indispensable to a man who regretted nothing in life so much as his own childlessness. Even Joe Strong, the debauched drunk, may have been useful to him as the antithesis of the virtuous clan chieftain he himself aspired to be. For better or worse, all the members of the family were mutually dependent in their geographical isolation. Since none of them could escape, every little domestic altercation – which in Europe or America could have been resolved by a shrug of the shoulders and a trip to a coffee-house – degenerated into a Homeric drama.

The unfortunate midpoint of this spider's web was Louis himself. Every one of its threads led from him and to him. He was the object of all desires, the butt of all rebellions, the addressee of all requests, the target of all unfulfilled hopes. He had to pay a particularly high price for his egotistical presumption in living under the same roof as three women. His mother Margaret was a paragon of genteel, lady-like Victorian restraint who avoided arguments, but Fanny and Belle were not only mother and daughter; they had the same pugnacious temperament and constantly vied for precedence as the patriarch's closest confidante. Forever at each other's throats, they shattered the rural hush with their shrill voices, burst into tears, hurled objects at walls. And it fell to Louis to restore domestic peace every time.

For decades, his biographers either made no mention of these dramas or confined themselves to vague allusions, a few for reasons of discretion but most because they did not know how fraught with violence the atmosphere at Vailima really was. This is because, in spite of their dissension, the family always drew a merciful veil of silence over these ugly scenes. Although Louis did pour out his heart to Sidney Colvin in one or two letters, his faithful friend carefully censored these before he published them.[6]

'I'll explain and expound a little bit,' Louis told Colvin in a censored passage dated 5 April 1893:

> We have a fly in the ointment here, it's not much but sufficiently annoying, and I am not always able, I am sorry to say, to behave well when the fly comes to the top. About one person you are to understand, and I cannot talk. I have often bad times, and have not borne it as I thought I might; it is a hard thing to bear perpetual quarrelling about *nix in creation*. Then there is another, who is an empty creature, and as good hearted as the empty can get to be. And between the two of them I get crazy. Person number one takes a tiff against person number two; person number two takes the day out crying; and then person number one, with characteristic generosity, comes to me (where she has been waiting half an hour before) and is in a dreadful state about person number two, whose condition is entirely of her own making. And my head and my heart are totally distraught between the pair of them. [...] There are certain words which drive me crazy when they recur. Is there a screw loose? Well, I suppose there is; but it's not really much and we'll manage (please God) to jog along.'[7]

It seems to have been mainly Fanny who was capable of working herself up into states so violent that Louis had on one occasion to summon Dr Funk from Apia in the middle of the night.

Later. 1.30. The doctor has been. 'There is no danger to life,' he said twice. – 'Is there any danger to mind?' I asked. – 'That is not excluded,' said he. Since then I have had a scene with which I need not harrow you; and now again she is quiet and seems without illusions. 'Tis a beastly business. [...] You see though I have written you so fully all these months, I have scarce been frank but kept my inmost trials to myself. At first it only seemed a kind of set against *me*; she made every talk an argument, then a quarrel; till I fled her, and lived in a kind of isolation in my own room. [...] The last was a hell of a scene which lasted all night. I will never tell anyone what about, it could not be believed, and was so unlike herself or any of us – in which Belle and I held her for about two hours; she wanted to run away. Then we took her to Sydney; and the first few weeks were delightful: her will quiet again – no more of that.[8]

No, it certainly wasn't the joys of enduring peace of mind that chained the Stevensons to their island paradise – far from it. In their heart of hearts, they all wanted to leave. Fanny was homesick for California. Belle yearned for the boulevards of Auckland and Sydney. Margaret Stevenson wanted to go back to Scotland. Louis and Lloyd were often away in any case, and young Austin was attending school by turns in San Francisco and Auckland. In all those years in Samoa, it very seldom happened that the entire family peacefully gathered together at Vailima. Even when they did, there would inevitably be one of those interminable domestic scenes that quite often ended only when visitors came and everyone had to mind their manners. One of the most frequent visitors was Louis's friend William Clarke, the missionary from the London Missionary Society who had mistaken the Stevensons for itinerant vaudeville artists when he witnessed their arrival. 'The excellent Clarke up here almost all day yesterday,' Louis wrote on 15 June 1892, 'a man I esteem and like to the soles of his boots; indeed I prefer him to any man in Samoa and most people in the world.'[9] This is profoundly illuminating: the person in Samoa dearest to him was neither his wife nor his stepdaughter nor his stepson, but William Clarke, the man with whom he had undertaken that mysterious boat trip during his first few days on the island.

In February 1893, after a particularly drastic family quarrel involving physical violence and hallucinations, Fanny, Belle and Louis fled their self-imposed prison and went aboard the *Mariposa,* which was bound for Australia. By the time they were two days into their holiday, all were perceptibly better. Louis, still weak after a bout of fever and two minor haemorrhages, was relieved to note that Fanny had polished off 'a whole fowl' for breakfast, 'to say nothing of a tower of hot cakes'.[10] When the three of them landed at Sydney after a two-week voyage of over 2,160 nautical miles, it signalled a return to civilization and the beginning of a resurrection that was to last three weeks. They stayed at the Oxford Hotel in King Street, where Louis was soon run to earth by journalists to whom he willingly granted hours-long interviews. He paid a visit to the university, inspected the Royal Mint and signed the visitors' book. He delivered a speech to the general assembly of the Presbyterian Church and addressed the local artists' association. He spent whole afternoons shopping with Fanny and Belle, slurped oysters and drank chilled champagne, and noticed to his amusement that people recognized him in the street. He had himself photographed at Kerry's' photographic studio and sat for a sculptor whose small bust of him did not meet with his entire satisfaction, 'but I mustn't criticize a present, and he had very little time to do it in. It is thought by my family to be a good likeness of Mark Twain.'[11]

On the return trip, just before the *Mariposa* entered Apia harbour, he wrote to his friend Colvin:

> Take it for all in all, it was huge fun: even Fanny had some lively sport at the beginning: Belle and I all through. We got Fanny a dress on the sly, made to fit Belle, gaudy black velvet and Duchesse lace. And alas! she was only able to wear it once. But we'll hope to see more of it at Samoa; it really is lovely. Both dames are royally outfitted in silk stockings, etc. We return, as from a raid, with our spoils and our wounded. [...] I am now very dandy; I announced two years ago that I should change. Slovenly youth, all right – not slovenly age. So really now I am pretty spruce: always a white shirt, white necktie, fresh shave, silk socks, O a great sight![12]

Every word of every line conveys how relieved the trio were to have escaped from their island prison at last, to have enjoyed the amenities of a British imperial city, to have mixed with people who spoke the same language and, above all, to have had a rest from each other. But then, after only three weeks, the fun came to an end and they re-embarked for Samoa aboard the *Mariposa*. One would dearly like to know why. It certainly can't have been the lure of Samoa that prompted their return, for they were scarcely back at Vailima before the everlasting round of illness and strife, recovery and reconciliation, hope and despair resumed its course.

Thursday, 5 April.[13] Well, there's no disguise possible: Fanny is not well, and we are miserably anxious. [...] You know about F there's nothing you can say is *wrong*, only it ain't *right*; it ain't *she*; at first she annoyed me dreadfully; now of course, that one understands, it is more anxious and pitiful.

Friday, 7 April. I am thankful to say the new medicine quieted her at once; and she has been entirely reasonable and very nice since she took it. A crape has been removed from the day for us. To make things better, the morning is ah! such a morning as you have never seen; heaven upon earth for sweetness, freshness, depth upon depth of unimaginable colour, and a huge silence broken at this moment only by the far-away murmur of the Pacific and the rich piping of a single bird. [...] You can't conceive what a relief this is. It seems a new world. She has such extraordinary recuperative power, that I do hope for the best. I am as tired as a man can be. This is a great trial to a family, and I thank God it seems as if ours was going to bear it well. And O! if it only lets up, it will be but a pleasant memory. We are all seedy, bar Lloyd: Fanny as per above; self nearly extinct; Belle, utterly overworked and bad toothache; Cook, down with a bad foot; Butler, prostrate with a bad leg. Eh, what a faim'ly! [sic].[14]

Divine Shenanigans

A T THE TIME the Stevensons were living in Samoa, peculiar things were happening on Cocos Eylandt, the peaceful volcanic island just below the horizon.[1] Tafahi's inhabitants, who for centuries had led a quiet life in the island's only village, forgotten by gods and men alike, were suddenly overcome with terror. The village, which was situated in the north just inland from the beach, comprised some 30 houses, none of which had walls. This was customary in the South Seas. For one thing, nobody owned anything that required protection from thieves; for another, the occupants were grateful for any cool breeze that relieved the heat and humidity beneath their palm-leaf roofs. It also meant that they could see from one end of the village to the other and share in their neighbours' family lives; and because they could do so, they did. It was impossible for anyone in this little community to keep a secret. If anything approached from the sea – a typhoon, a flock of birds, a ship – all the villagers spotted it from a long way off.

One day towards the end of the 19th century, something awe-inspiring and unprecedented bore down on the island. Resembling a ship in appearance, it emitted shafts of lightning and claps of thunder as it drew nearer. Curiously, it didn't go ashore at the north of the island, the only safe landing place, but at the other end, on a lonely beach in the uninhabited south. The people of Tafahi had never before seen a creature that gave off thunder and lightning, so there was great agitation in the village. The women wailed, the children wept, the men looked grim. Many of the villagers ran off and hid in the jungle, but Chief Maatu kept his head and conferred with Tou-maama, his medicine man. To the latter, the answer was obvious: the phenomenon was clearly not of human or natural origin, so it had to be a divine manifestation. And, since the deity had approached Tafahi from the north, it had to be Fatuulu the fish-god, because Fatuulu was the only one out of all the Tongan gods who lived so far to the north, on a small rock halfway to Samoa.

It seems that the medicine man set off boldly for the south of the island, all by himself, to fulfil his mission as a mediator between gods and men. There he discovered that the fish-god had gone ashore and assumed human form. Hurrying back to the village, he informed its inhabitants that the fish-god would tolerate no mortal in his vicinity save Toumaama himself; that no one else was permitted to see him; and that anyone who ventured into the fish-god's sphere of operations, the small strip of sand in the south, would instantly drop dead.

One would naturally like to know what form of arcane activity the fish-god was pursuing in solitude – for instance, whether he had a pick and shovel with him and whether he disappeared into the jungle behind the beach, possibly guided by a scrap of paper. The medicine man maintained his professional discretion, however, so the secret never came out. None of the villagers, not even Chief Maatu, ever discovered what was going on in the south. After a few days or weeks Fatuulu left the way he had come. Heading north to a renewed accompaniment of much thunder and lightning, he disappeared in the direction of Samoa. For a while the villagers continued to engage in excited debate and speculation. A few daring souls may even have made an excursion to the south, but they found nothing worth mentioning, either on the virginal sandy beach or among the coconut palms on the steep, jungle-clad slopes behind it. So they shrugged their shoulders and dismissed the matter from their minds.

The dust had scarcely settled, however, when the fish-god returned to another salvo of thunder and lightning. On this occasion, too, he spent some time ashore before disappearing once more – only to turn up yet again a little while later. Fatuulu came and went every few weeks, just as he pleased. Every time the fish-god appeared Toumaama would go into a trance and tremble all over like a leaf in the wind. He wouldn't eat, his face glowed, his eyes glazed over. From their hiding-places the villagers would then hear Fatuulu bellowing orders – by way of their priest's lips – in a voice so superhumanly loud that it could be heard on the neighbouring island of Niuatoputapu 5½ miles away. Sometimes he would command them to slaughter a pig for him.

What strikes one is that Fatuulu's love of such earthly shenanigans was rather atypical. All the other members of the Tongan pantheon tended to devote themselves to activities of a conventionally divine nature. They spread the vault of heaven over the earth, controlled the movements of stars and birds and shoals of fish, adjusted the interplay of wind and weather, and concerned themselves with ocean currents and the fertility of women and gardens. Of all the Tongan gods, Fatuulu was the only one to walk on sandy beaches in human guise, experience an occasional hankering for roast pork and amuse himself by terrifying mortals with thunder and lightning. Why he should have chosen that stretch of beach was a big mystery. Devoid of religious significance, it was merely a narrow strip of white sand between the water and the steep, jungle-clad slopes. The only feature worth mentioning was a big black rock, which became known henceforth as 'Fatuulu's Rock'. The ground around it was sacred. Whoever set foot on it would drop dead. Not even Chief Maatu dared to do so.

However, there was little danger that anyone would drop dead because the islanders continued to live as they had lived from time immemorial: in the immediate vicinity of their village, where their fields and fishing grounds were. They had no reason to visit the beach in the south; there was no fertile soil there and the fishing was poor. It made no difference to their daily lives that the fish-god forbade them to do what they never did in any case, so they gradually became accustomed to his visits. They no longer took fright when he passed by, flashing and roaring and bellowing; they merely paused in their work, leant on their spades, and waved to him like an old friend.

But at some stage – exactly when cannot be ascertained – it struck someone that Fatuulu had not passed by for quite a while. The puzzled islanders kept watch on the sea for several months. Then, with another shrug of the shoulders, they decided that the fish-god must have been detained for some reason or was now visiting some other island. Village life was so taken up with births and weddings and deaths that Fatuulu eventually became forgotten.

12

Thunder and Lightning

THAT THE INHABITANTS of Tafahi should have been so fright-ened by a little thunder and lightning and bellowing was understandable. In those days their island was very remote from the pandemonium of the modern world. Even the inhabitants of neighbouring Samoa would have been only half as agitated; there, every child realized that thunder and lightning were not necessarily of meteorological or divine origin but could also be occasioned by fireworks. In earlier years, missionaries used to let off rockets when nearing the islands of Samoa to overawe the inhabitants. In 1891 Stevenson's friend William Clarke went a step further by writing several letters to the headquarters of the London Missionary Society requesting it to finance the purchase of as powerful a magic lantern as possible, so that he could project pictures on the jungle. When the treasurer finally, after much hesitation, approved a grant of £25, Clarke ordered a projector from Glasgow together with glass slides of Queen Victoria and all manner of princes and presidents. One can well imagine what a terrifying spectacle their much-magnified figures must have made when projected on to a South Seas jungle at night.

The Samoans had also been inured to superhuman bellowing ever since Louis's friend Harry J Moors imported the first Edison loud-speaker and music box. Thomas Alva Edison had invented the sound transformer – a non-electrical loudspeaker – in 1870 and the phono-graph in 1877. The latter had come on the market in 1887, three years before the Stevensons arrived in Samoa.

Where thunder and lightning are concerned, Fanny's diary contains an interesting anecdote. She sailed to Australia and New Zealand with her husband and son a few days after Louis bought

Vailima, and they purchased a large quantity of fireworks and ammunition in Auckland on the return trip.

> Lloyd was a little doubtful about the calcium fire and questioned
> the man at the chemist shop rather closely, particularly as to its
> inflammability, explaining that it was to be carried on board ship. The
> man declared that it was perfectly safe, 'as safe,' said he, 'as a packet of
> sugar,' adding that fire from a match would not be sufficient to ignite
> it. 'Will you have it with or without fumes?' he asked as he turned to
> make up the parcel. [...] We left Auckland last evening at about eight,
> the streaming lights from the town following us a long way. [...] I sat
> at the saloon table eating brown bread and butter. Suddenly, from the
> cabin occupied by Tin Jack and Lloyd, came a spitting puff, almost
> immediately followed by gorgeous flames and the most horrible
> chemical stench. The calcium fire that was as safe as a packet of sugar
> had gone off and ignited the rest of the fireworks. Only Lloyd and
> I knew of the cartridges in their midst, but we discreetly held our
> tongues, though every moment we expected to hear the ping of flying
> bullets. I ran into our cabin and snatched a heavy red blanket. Louis,
> who knew nothing of the fireworks having been brought on board, was
> thunderstruck by the vivid changing colours of the spouts of flame, and
> stood for some time gazing at the extraordinary scene and inhaling the
> poisonous vapours. 'Why,' he thought with wonder, 'should a fire at sea
> look like a Christmas pantomime?'[1]

One thing emerges from this conjunction of circumstances: at the very least, we cannot preclude the possibility that Fatuulu the fish-god was none other than Robert Louis Stevenson. On the contrary, it is quite conceivable that he made a surprising discovery during his first few days in Samoa: that Tafahi was once known as Cocos Eylandt. Perhaps, during that first boat trip in December 1889, William Clarke showed him an old chart on which the former name still appeared. Either that, or Louis himself discovered this in course of his own research, perhaps in conversation with the German, British or American consul. It must then have occurred to him that generations of treasure-hunters had been looking for the Lima Treasure on the wrong island. If he did indeed come to that conclusion, it is obvious that he would have wanted to postpone his return to Scotland for a while and explore the place in person.

Unlike the first Cocos Island, the second had the disadvantage of being inhabited. The kings and princes of Tonga had always enjoyed a reputation for being warlike rulers who guarded their possessions jealously. It would have been quite impossible for the Stevensons to land on Tafahi and engage in an overt search for treasure. Samoa, on the other hand, was only a day's voyage away and inhabited by an eccentric community of 300 Europeans who had dropped anchor there for a wide variety of more or less plausible reasons. The family could unobtrusively make their home there; not in the middle of Apia, which was swarming with inquisitive loafers, but not too far from it either, so that supplies could be obtained. In that respect, Vailima was the ideal spot.

Having acquired a discreet base of operations, Louis had to ensure that his friends and relations at home in Scotland didn't smell a rat. He had to produce convincing reasons for settling in Samoa permanently, hence his allusions to the agreeable climate, the sudden improvement in his health, the beauty of the tropical scenery and the joys of agricultural self-sufficiency.

If he was contemplating frequent trips by sea, Apia harbour would naturally be very useful to him. On the other hand, harbours are the worst possible places in which to keep a secret. Every incoming and outgoing vessel is the cynosure of a hundred pairs of eyes, has to report on arrival and departure, pay harbour dues and render an account of its passengers and cargo. Although Louis could doubtless have sneaked out of the harbour once or twice aboard some boat or other, he could never have made regular trips to an unknown destination in a boat of his own and escaped notice – unless he didn't put to sea from Apia at all, but from a beach in some small, secluded cove, preferably aboard one of those graceful Samoan outriggers capable of crossing the reef to the open sea and covering the 166 miles to Tafahi at twice the speed of any European craft.

Anyone undertaking a voyage to the south would have chosen to set sail from the south coast, thereby avoiding curious eyes and a long, dangerous detour along the reef around the island. It was a great advantage that the only route leading south across the island from Apia passed barely 220 yards east of the Stevenson property. If Louis urged his docile little horse Jack into a trot, he could easily cover the 9.3 miles to the south coast in three hours. The Cross Island Road, which is still the principal north-south route across Samoa's main island, was developed into a road five years after his death by the German colonial administration.

Louis would seldom have made the trip on his own. His stepson Lloyd may have accompanied him, or possibly William Clarke or Harry Moors, and there would certainly have been a Samoan crew of five to eight men on board. It is also conceivable that some expeditions took place without Louis when he was confined to bed by one of his numerous spells of ill health. It may then have been Lloyd who acted as his right-hand man, lit the 'calcium fire' on approaching Tafahi and set up the Edison equipment. Lloyd often went away on trips by himself. He sometimes claimed to have gone skating in New Zealand, or surfing in Hawaii, or amusing himself in San Francisco. On other occasions he made no mention of where he was going. What strikes one about these excursions is that there are no independent accounts of them and hardly any photographs.

In addition to Lloyd Osbourne, Harry Moors and William Clarke, there was a fourth potential treasure-hunter: Louis's Scottish cousin Graham Balfour, who first visited Vailima in 1892. A qualified lawyer of 34, Balfour was a tall, high-spirited fellow with a fair moustache. He was also unmarried, which explains why Belle, recently divorced, was quick to fall in love with him. He did not, however, reciprocate her feelings and moved into Lloyd's bachelor quarters. Although he had originally intended to stay only a month, Vailima became his base for some years, and it was from there that he undertook various largely undocumented excursions into the South Seas.

Landing on the south coast of Tafahi is not easy. To cross the reef and enter the quiet lagoon would have required great skill on the part of the Samoan boatmen. It is quite possible that the prominent black rock the islanders were soon to christen 'Fatuulu's Rock' served them as a landmark. Once ashore the men would have dug in the sand, spent days or weeks searching the steep volcanic slopes and the shoreline near the water's edge, and, in the evenings, dined on roast pork ordered from the natives by means of their loudspeaker. When their supplies ran out, they would have returned to Samoa, where Louis resumed his authorial activities. He never said another word about pirates or treasure islands during those years. When he did write stories about the South Seas, he always stressed that they had occurred to him out of the blue. It is interesting, however, that *The Beach of Falesá,* written in 1892, features a white adventurer and ne'er-do-well named Case, who goes about his nefarious business in a secluded bay and keeps the superstitious natives away by suspending wooden crates fitted with mandolin strings in the trees. The weird aeolian music made by the wind as it stirs the strings fills the islanders with nameless dread.

It is quite possible that Louis's exertions on this second Cocos Island were as fruitless as those of August Gissler and a thousand treasure-hunters before and after him on the first. If he really did find any gold and silver or precious stones, he would have loaded the boat with as much treasure as possible – the Samoans' frail-looking but remarkably strong outriggers can carry cargoes of several hundred-weight – and conveyed it across the sea to Vailima. He would then have waited a few weeks before returning – to the accompaniment of more thunder and lightning – and loading up again. The huge safe that still stands in the spacious hall at Vailima could have held a cargo or two of gold and precious stones. But it could not have been Louis's intention simply to transport the Lima Treasure from Tafahi to Samoa, that is to say, from one island to another. No treasure-hunter would have grown rich by hanging on to a hoard of Spanish doubloons. In order to enjoy the fruits of his good fortune, he would have had to turn the gold into money, in other words, transform doubloons into dollars and treasure chests into bank accounts. Apia had one or two traders – Harry Moors among them, of course – who offered banking facilities, but if Robert Louis Stevenson had wanted to convert large quantities of pirate gold he would have more likely sought the discreet assistance of major banking houses in cities where not too many questions would be asked about the source of such assets. For reasons of security and discretion it might also have been sensible not to convey the whole hoard to a bank at one fell swoop – possibly via a fence or a goldsmith with a sufficiently capacious smelting furnace – but to distribute it in small quantities among several banks. In that event, regular visits to Sydney, Auckland or Honolulu would have been necessary. The members of the Stevenson clan did, in fact, go on a remarkable number of shortish voyages during their five years in Samoa.

1890: Louis twice visits Sydney and Auckland for no stated reason. Fanny makes the 621-mile trip to the Fiji Islands to engage a cook. Lloyd is sent to England to fetch some furniture.

1891: Louis goes to Sydney to collect his mother and Lloyd, who have arrived there from England. Lloyd goes on numerous trips thereafter, destinations unknown.

1892: Louis's cousin Graham Balfour arrives. Based at Vailima for the

next two years, he undertakes numerous voyages in the South
Seas. Belle's son Austin Strong goes off to school in Monterey,
California, returning to Samoa for the holidays.

February 1893: Louis, Fanny and Belle sail to Sydney for a holiday.

September 1893: Louis goes to Hawaii.

October 1893: Fanny collects Louis from Hawaii.

May 1894: Lloyd goes to New Zealand to skate.

December 1894: Lloyd goes away on holiday shortly after Louis's
death.

It must also be said that undeclared pirate treasure constituted
illegal assets even in the 19th century, so the fortunate finder had
to try to conceal its provenance by cloaking it in a credible myth of
legality. Today this process is known as money-laundering. Corrupt
politicians, drug and arms dealers and white-collar criminals go to
great lengths to invest their dirty money in legal but opaque businesses. Many buy paintings by Gauguin or Van Gogh, whose real
worth no one knows, others buy footballers or whole football teams
or casinos. Then they pay tax on huge profits they never really aimed
to make, with the result that previously illegal assets now acquire a
legal, if mythical, provenance. The number of those in the know must
be kept to a minimum. If they become too numerous it sometimes
happens that one or another of them dies an untimely death.

Most of these tricks were impracticable in Robert Louis Stevenson's day. The art trade was in its infancy; when he settled in Samoa,
Van Gogh had just made his one and only sale (*The Red Vineyard*
for 400 francs) and Gauguin would not pay his first visit to Tahiti
until 1891. As for football, it was still an amateur game throughout
the world. But vast sums of suspect money were disappearing into
real estate and yielding huge profits at the end of the 19th century,
notably in the western United States. And those profits were multiplied many times over in the 20th century, when oil was discovered
beneath the properties in question.

That, therefore, is the route the Lima Treasure might have taken if
Robert Louis Stevenson actually recovered it on Tafahi. And lo! As
we shall see in due course, the Stevenson clan went into Californian
real estate when their South Seas adventure ended; secondly, oil is
said to have been discovered on one of their properties; and, thirdly, a
remarkable number of clan members died untimely deaths from very
similar causes – until, in the end, only one of them was left.

13

The Pirates' Island

IN SEPTEMBER 1893, Louis took off on another of his surprising trips for no plausible reason. Simply 'for the sake of the voyage',[1] he boarded the mailboat SS *Mariposa* at Apia and sailed 2,796 miles north to Hawaii, which he reached a week later. With him were his cousin Graham Balfour and his Samoan manservant Ta'alolo. They had planned to return home by the next steamer after a week's stay, but Ta'alolo developed measles on the voyage. The Hawaiian authorities allowed him to go ashore on 20 September but placed him in quarantine. While Louis and Graham put up at the Sans Souci Hotel on Waikiki Beach, Ta'alolo was housed in a secluded beach hut nearby, closely supervised by a guard to ensure that he did not escape and received no visitors.

Louis enjoyed this return to civilization. He hired a cabby for the entire duration of his stay and had himself driven from one social function to another. He called on Queen Lilioukulani, who had just been deposed, addressed the Scottish Thistle Club, an association of Scottish expatriates, and – as ever – held court for journalists. If reporters did not visit him at his hotel, he went to their newspaper offices. The day before he was due to return to Samoa, however, he developed an inflammation of the lungs and a high fever, probably accompanied by his 'old friend blood-spitting'. A sea voyage being out of the question, he sent for Dr Trousseau, the best-known doctor in Hawaii, and gave the *Mariposa* a telegram asking Fanny to collect him from Honolulu.

George Philippe Trousseau was a 60-year-old Frenchman. He acted as personal physician to the Hawaiian royal family, had functioned for many years as Honolulu's epidemiologist and port physician, ran an ostrich farm and sugar plantation, and raised sheep on the side. If he missed anything in Hawaii, it was erudite conversation with people of his own social status and education, so he much enjoyed having Robert Louis Stevenson as his patient. On his daily visits to Sans Souci, he would pull up a chair beside the celebrated author's bed, light a cigar, and spend an hour or two discussing literature with him. One day he suggested that his patient should write a Polynesian story in verse. Louis replied that a good story couldn't withstand the constraints of verse form. Having learnt Latin and Greek at school in Paris, Dr Trousseau refused to accept this affront to hexameters and pentameters and urged him at least to try. Still weak with fever, Louis wouldn't climb down. 'Well,' he said eventually, 'shall I try right here?' Taking pencil and paper, he told Trousseau to keep quiet until he'd finished his cigar. Half an hour later he handed the doctor a sheet of paper bearing an account of a voyage in verse:

The Pirates' Island

'Twas on a Monday evening we sailed forth,
And veered into the purple and the gold
Of our warm Southern sea. We were but six –
Four stalwart natives and two whites – who sailed
Upon that unknown course. Never had they,
My brown Samoans, ventured so; nor would
Have ventured now, had I not been with them
To urge hearts on. When we had been five days
Or more upon the main, and yet no land
Or atoll came in sight, I knew that we
Had missed our port, for on my chart there lay,
Across our course, the sea-famed island where.
'Twas said by ancient chiefs, great treasure lay,
Hidden long years ago by pirates bold,
Who seized the lumb'ring carracks (from the Isle
of Spices) coming far from o'er the sea.
And on this flitting isle Samoans say,
Within a hollow mountain near the shore,
Were hid cargoes full of bright shining gold
In lumps and wedges, fit for kingly state;
With black and yellow pearls for Chieftain's ears,

From the warm seas that wash the shores of Ind.
It was this tale that since their childhood's day
Had pricked their curiosity, and made
Them bold to rove; to leave the cava bowl,
The bursting bread-fruit, and the luscious gold
Of rip'ning plantains, to follow o'er the weaves,
That chance might bring them to wealth, or death – or both.
So when I told them, 'Children, we are lost!'
The lad Upolu fell to wailing in
The native way, until Chief Kimo sternly said,
'Now hush thee, silly one, or thou wilt shame
Thy parents and thy tribe. Let not ...' [2]

The fragment breaks off at this point. At the very bottom of the sheet Louis wrote:

Sir, this is not first chop, but it is enough. You will see that prose is the best by long odds for story-tellers who depend on realistic action for their interest. You may preserve this as a sample of how the plausible suggestions of our well-meaning friends may fail in practice. I sign myself, sir, Your obedient servant, R. L. S.

The fragment remained in George Philippe Trousseau's private possession. For whatever reason or reasons, it has never been included in the official editions of Robert Louis Stevenson's works.

14

Do I Look Strange?

THE LAST DAY of Louis's life was 3 December 1894. He had as usual started work just before 6 a.m., when everyone else at Vailima was asleep; that is to say, he sat up in bed, propped his back against some pillows, took pencil and paper, and proceeded to rough out the ninth chapter of his latest novel, *The Weir of Hermiston,* which was never finished. An hour later a servant would have brought him an orange for breakfast, and two hours after that Belle turned up to take dictation. In the afternoon he went for a dip in the small pond behind the house, which the family used as a swimming pool, and when the sun dipped below the mountain he went upstairs to his bedroom to change for dinner. He came downstairs shortly after 6 p.m. to find Fanny out on the veranda in the darkest of moods. Having for days been haunted by a terrible presentiment that something bad would happen to one of her nearest and dearest, she felt positive that it would be Graham Balfour, who was once again away at sea. Louis tried to distract her with cheerful banter, coaxed her into playing a hand of cards, and suggested that they have a 'Vailima salad' for supper. He fetched a bottle of burgundy and busied himself with the salad, for which he mixed a dressing of olive oil and lime juice. Suddenly he clutched his head and cried: 'What's that! What a pain! Do I look strange?' Fanny concealed her alarm and said no, but he 'reeled and fell backwards'. Fanny and her manservant Sosimo helped him into the house and sat him down in his favourite green armchair beside the fireplace, which had once belonged to his grandfather Robert Stevenson, the inventor of the flashing lighthouse. Belle and his mother, Margaret, were summoned, and Lloyd came hurrying over from his bachelor quarters. Louis, slumped in the armchair with his eyes wide open, was breathing stertorously. Fanny kept calling his name, but he gave no sign of recognition. The women asked that a camp bed be brought, and Lloyd and Sosimo hoisted him on to it. When Fanny, Belle and Margaret made to remove his riding boots, Lloyd protested that he had always said he wanted to die with his boots on. However, they considered rendering first aid preferable to the literal and premature fulfilment of Louis's last wish, so Lloyd was dispatched to Apia to summon every available doctor. Dr Bernhard Funk of the Deutsche Handelsgesellschaft diagnosed an apoplectic fit occasioned by a blood clot in the brain; Dr Robert W Andersen from HMS *Wallaroo* diagnosed a cerebral haemorrhage. Fanny vainly tried to revive her husband by chafing his arms with brandy. When Anderson saw his emaciated limbs, he blurted out, 'How can anyone write books with those arms?' Fanny retorted, 'He has written all his books with those arms.'

Louis's best friend, the missionary William Clarke, turned up soon after the doctors. They all stood round the deathbed. Fanny and Belle continued their attempts to stimulate the dying man's circulation with brandy. Lloyd held him in his arms, Margaret and Clarke knelt beside the bed and prayed as his breathing grew steadily weaker. At ten past eight it ceased altogether.

Fanny knew that the body would have to be buried no later than the following afternoon because decomposition sets in so quickly in the tropics. It was also clear that Louis must be buried on Mount Vaea, in accordance with his wishes. There was no path to the summit, so Fanny sent her servants to the surrounding villages to ask the chiefs to clear one before the night was out. At once, 200 men hurried to the scene and spread out along the whole route from Vailima to the summit. Then they set to work with machetes, pickaxes, shovels, mattocks and crowbars. Throughout the night, Vailima's occupants could hear muffled shouts, the crash of falling trees and the Latin prayers the house boys had been taught by missionaries. Those labourers who had cleared their stretch of the route made their way either to the summit to carve out a clearing for the grave, or down to the beach to fetch crushed white coral and black lava, in which Samoan kings and senior chiefs were traditionally buried. Meanwhile, the servants rubbed Louis's body with coconut oil scented with perfume distilled from the flowers of the ylang-ylang tree (*Canagium odoratum*). He was not, however, wrapped in finely woven mats in conformity with Samoan custom, but laid in a coffin in the European manner. This was made on the spot during the night by Alex Willis, a carpenter from Apia, who wept as he bent over the corpse to measure it. Then Louis was dressed in his velvet jacket and a Union Jack was draped over his emaciated form.

When the sun was at its zenith the following day, the path was finished and the funeral procession began its arduous ascent. The senior chief took the lead followed by his deputy, who blew long, resonant notes on a conch. Then came the coffin, which was carefully passed from hand to hand by men stationed in groups of four all the way up the steep slope. The path, whose surface consisted of damp soil and slippery lava scree, was flanked by ferns and bushes dripping with moisture. Margaret and Fanny soon grew tired and had to turn back. The rest took an hour to reach the open grave on the small plateau at the summit. The Reverend William Clarke conducted the burial service and read a prayer composed by Louis himself. Then four Samoans standing in the grave took the coffin and laid it down on its bed of lava and coral. Having buried it beneath a mound of earth, they covered that, too, with black lava. Last of all, they drove a stake into the ground and attached a little metal cross to it. So that Louis could rest in peace, the chiefs ordained that the discharging of firearms on Mount Vaea be prohibited for evermore.[1]

15

The Bottle Imp Emigrates

DEPRIVED OF THEIR SOLE BREADWINNER, Fanny, Belle, Lloyd and Austin remained at Vailima on their own. It seemed unlikely that any of them would ever earn a substantial amount of money. Austin, now 13 years old, was a very mediocre scholar of no special talent. Fanny and Belle had always had a male breadwinner and were chronically extravagant. As for Lloyd Osbourne, he was preoccupied with parties, holiday trips, billiard tournaments and native girls. Financially, as regards both income and expenditure, he would have been extremely surprised to be asked to engage in paid work.

The only person at Vailima who really did have money was Louis's mother, Margaret, who managed the Stevensons' family fortune. However, a few days after her son's death she decided to go home to Scotland and spend her declining years in Edinburgh with her sister, Jane Whyte Balfour. Pneumonia carried her off two years later. In her delirium she saw her only son standing at the foot of her bed. 'There's Louis! I must go!' she cried, and died the next day.

Nevertheless, it is an interesting fact that none of the remaining occupants of Vailima was ever faced with the unpleasant necessity of having to work for money. Harry Moors had no cause for complaint either; his business enterprises prospered so well that he continued to be Samoa's biggest individual taxpayer until his death 32 years later. It is also noteworthy that Louis's best friend, William Clarke, left the mission immediately after the author's death and travelled back to Britain with Margaret Stevenson.*

---

*'To me, Mr Stevenson's death has been a terrible blow,' Clarke wrote to his London headquarters on 25 January 1895. 'He treated me as a brother, and I

It was as if the Bottle Imp in Louis's story had decided to go on attending to the family's welfare. Whisky and burgundy continued to flow like water, servants continued to perform the menial household chores, and visitors to Vailima were as royally entertained as ever. In quest of relaxation after the exertions of the funeral, Lloyd treated himself to a brief sea voyage. Scarcely had he returned when he joined Fanny and Belle on a trip to California. On the way back they spent three months in Hawaii, where they stayed at the Hotel Sans Souci on Waikiki Beach. By the time they returned to Vailima a whole year had elapsed since Louis's death. When the news of Margaret Stevenson's death reached them after another year the Osbournes turned their backs on Vailima for ever and left for Scotland to take up the Stevenson inheritance. Fanny casually sold the property for £1,750, less than one-fifth of the sum Louis had spent on buying the land and building the house. The purchaser was a retired Hamburg businessman named Gustav Kunst, who had made a fortune out of the Trans-Siberian Railway and the fur trade.[*]

Fanny underwent an astonishing transformation in the years that followed. Having constantly suffered from all manner of imaginary and genuine illnesses and indispositions, she now enjoyed the best of health and good spirits. She bought a big automobile in which she and Lloyd gadded around France, Spain and Portugal. She spent an

---

loved him dearly. [...] I have lost my best and kindest friend in Samoa, and I feel thankful that it is in the pathway of my duty to turn my steps homewards to those who alone are dearer to me. Mrs Stevenson senior will probably accompany us to England.' The Clarkes did, in fact, sail for England with Margaret Stevenson on 21 February 1895, arriving there on 8 May. On 14 April 1917, 22 years later, Clarke set off for Samoa once more – alone this time. He remained there for two years and undertook numerous trips by sea. On 7 August 1920 he returned to London, where he died on 25 May 1922.

[*] In his latter years, Gustav Kunst (*c*.1836–1905) fled the European winters for German Samoa, where he gained a reputation for philanthropy by building Apia a covered market and a hospital for the white inhabitants. After he died, his nephew sold Vailima to the German government, which converted it into the governor's residence. In 1914, when New Zealand troops expelled the German colonists from Samoa at the outbreak of the First World War, it was taken over by the New Zealand governor. After Samoa gained its independence in 1962, Vailima became the residence of the Samoan head of state. Very badly damaged by hurricanes in 1990 and 1991, the building was bought by US investors associated with the Mormon Church and converted into the Robert Louis Stevenson Museum.

agreeable winter in Madeira and built herself a fortress-like residence overlooking San Francisco, which she furnished with Stevenson antiques shipped over from Samoa. In the evenings she used to sit on the terrace and watch ships passing under Golden Gate Bridge on their way out into the Pacific. She also attended spiritualist meetings in the hope of making contact with Louis beyond the grave.

That the Osbournes were able to afford such a luxurious lifestyle is somewhat surprising. It is true that Louis had earned a great deal of money from his writing, and that his paternal forebears had made a substantial fortune out of their lighthouses, but the clan had led an expensive existence during his lifetime. Moreover, his estate had been divided up among so many beneficiaries that it would not have sufficed to keep them in idle affluence for decades.*

When Fanny was 64 and Louis had been dead ten years, another man turned up at her side. She engaged a 'private secretary' in the person of a shy but well-educated and amusing young journalist whose job it was to take care of all the practical aspects of her daily life. Edward 'Ned' Field kept Fanny's books, managed her bank accounts, dealt with the tax inspector, booked ship's passages and hotel rooms and reserved tables for her in restaurants. He was her '*homme de confiance*'. Although 40 years her junior, he came, like her, from Indianapolis, where his mother and Fanny had gone to school together. Their relationship soon became decidedly intimate. The young man never left her side by day or night, nor even at weekends. This gave rise to a certain amount of whispering, but when the ill-matched couple took to going on long trips to New York, Mexico and Europe together, the state of affairs seemed so obvious that all whispers ceased.

Ned faithfully accompanied Fanny on all her travels until 17 February 1914, when the two of them were sitting in their living-room on the heights above San Francisco. Fanny leafed through some magazines, then played a hand of cards with Ned as darkness enshrouded the fruit trees outside, which were white with blossom. At half past ten Fanny went to bed. At some point during the night she was

---

*Under the terms of Louis's last will, dated September 1893, a quarter of his paternal estate, which his mother Margaret had administered, went to his cousin Bob (£3,136) and the latter's sisters Dora Fowke and Katharine de Mattos (£1,568 each). A quarter of the residue (£4,704) was to be invested for Belle. The remainder (£14,112), which went to Fanny, was to pass to Lloyd on her death.[1]

carried off by a stroke – just as Louis had been 19 years, two months and two weeks before her.

Fanny's body was cremated after a simple funeral service. Her last will stipulated that her ashes should be buried beside Robert Louis Stevenson's remains on the summit of Mount Vaea. Belle agreed to travel to Samoa with her mother's urn. Before leaving, however, she did something remarkable: she not only inherited her mother's estate – subject to paying Lloyd a monthly allowance of $300 – but took over the '*homme de confiance*' who had managed the family's financial affairs for over ten years. On 19 August 1914, six months after Fanny's death, Isobel Strong Osbourne and Edward Salisbury Field were married at Los Gatos, Santa Clara County, California. She was 56 years old and he 35 – exactly the same age as her son Austin Strong, whose stepfather he now became. It was as if the Bottle Imp had passed from Fanny to her daughter.

Belle's second marriage was as happy as her first had been miserable. For the first time in her life she made a lot of money, auctioning off masses of Stevenson's letters, notes and unpublished manuscripts. Ned proved a faithful and affectionate husband, and she looked after the shy young man like a wise and far-sighted mother. At her instigation he abandoned journalism in favour of novels and humorous stage plays.* Above all, though, he speculated in real estate, for which he appears to have had a definite flair.

Sadly, Ned Field died an untimely death on 18 September 1936, Belle's 78th birthday, at their country house on the shores of Zaca Lake, a tranquil stretch of water in the wilds north of Santa Barbara. The couple had enjoyed a festive birthday lunch on their own. Afterwards, Ned lay down for a siesta and never woke up. He died quite unexpectedly at the age of only 56. Belle's composure was remarkable under the circumstances. The elderly lady dragged her dead husband to the car, hefted him on to the back seat and drove him home to Santa Barbara, 35 miles away.[2]

This was not the last death Belle had to mourn – the price most long-lived people have to pay for their good fortune. On 22 May 1947

---

*Ned Fields's greatest successes were the comedies *Twin Beds* (1914) and *Wedding Bells* (1919). According to the *New York Times,* the first dealt mainly with 'pajamas and peignoirs, trousers and truculence, females and fight'. Of the second, Alexander Woolcott, writing in *The Times,* said it was 'a sprightly and diverting farce' which had 'a nice vein of nonsense running through it'.

she found herself sitting beside the deathbed of her younger brother Lloyd in Los Angeles. Lloyd had spent his entire life in the smartest clubs and bars in Paris, London and New York. To the last, he remained the self-centred dandy he had been at Vailima. In 1896 he had married a pretty and intelligent girl named Katherine Durham, who bore him two sons: Alan in 1897 and Louis in 1900. However, his mother and his wife were at daggers drawn. When Fanny presented him with a choice between leaving Katherine and forgoing his inheritance, he opted for the former. He went on numerous cruises and maintained bank accounts in various countries and liked buying expensive cars. He also, during the 1930s, developed a predilection for the Nazi love of order and the political ideas of Benito Mussolini. He married Yvonne Payerne, a Frenchwoman 40 years his junior, who bore him another son, and spent his declining years on the Côte d'Azur. By the time he returned to the United States to die it was too late for a reconciliation with the family. His first wife and his sons Alan and Louis declined to bid him farewell on his deathbed.[3]

So Isobel Osbourne Strong Field became a lonely old woman. She was left completely alone on 17 September 1952, the day before her 94th birthday, when her only child Austin Strong – who had defied all predictions by making quite a career for himself as a Broadway playwright* – died at his holiday home in Nantucket at the age of 71. But there was yet another quirk of fate in store for Belle. Quite unexpectedly – or so runs the family legend handed down by generations of biographers – substantial deposits of oil were found on several of the properties she had inherited from Ned Field. Allegedly situated at Long Beach and Signal Hill, south of Los Angeles, these oil wells proved so miraculously productive that Belle, Vailima's last heiress, ended her days a fabulously wealthy woman. It was as if the Bottle Imp had rendered the Osbournes a final service.

It is a fact that one of the biggest oilfields in North America was discovered at Long Beach in 1921, or 15 years before Ned Field's death. Hundreds of small landowners hurriedly erected thousands of little derricks for fear their neighbours might drain off the oil beneath

---

*Austin Strong's most successful play by far was *Seventh Heaven,* a romantic comedy which opened on Broadway on 30 October 1922 and ran for 704 performances. It was filmed in 1927 with Janet Gaynor and Charles Farrell in the leading roles. This silent film was followed in 1937 by a talkie starring Simone Simon and James Stewart.

their properties. The oilfield really did prove productive – oil still gushes from it to this day – and many landowners really did become wealthy. However, there is no documentary evidence that a man named Ned Field was one of their fortunate number. The records of the Department of Oil Properties at Long Beach list no one of that name, nor does the Los Angeles Basin Geological Society.

Isobel Osbourne Strong Field died at Santa Barbara, California, on 26 June 1953. She was buried at Forest Lawn Memorial Park in Glendale. With her, Vailima's last inhabitant and Robert Louis Stevenson's last confidante went to the grave.

The Breath that Came from the Sea

So what remains now that all are dead? There remain the two Cocos Islands. Serenely situated amid the Pacific breakers, they continue to guard their secret and, over and above that, the secret of whether their secret has ever been plumbed. Even though they remain untouched by dramas of human passion and greed, they are far from immobile. On the contrary, geology teaches us that volcanic islands are extremely unstable tectonic structures. They are subject to displacement and eruptions and extremely violent earthquakes; new land emerges from the waves, whole promontories sink beneath them. Moreover, the level of the Pacific is slowly but steadily rising as the polar ice caps melt. If one compares the oldest extant maps of the Cocos Islands with the latest satellite photographs, it is clear that their present outlines bear little resemblance to those of two centuries ago. Neither Captain Thompson nor John Keating nor Robert Louis Stevenson would be able to find their way around – not even with the aid of the map which Thompson may have drawn on the day he buried the treasure. It seems very probable that, unless someone has unearthed it at some stage, all the gold and silver has been abraded by the immense forces prevailing in the depths of a volcanic island. The treasure may also have sunk into the sea or been vaporized by the heat of molten lava ...

None of this has deterred generations of treasure-hunters from passing on the spade, so to speak, though only on the Costa Rican Cocos Island. Tafahi, by contrast, has regained its paradisal tranquillity since the days of Robert Louis Stevenson and Fatuulu the fish-god. In the last few decades the inhabitants have been planting best quality vanilla, for which they obtain high prices on the world market. None of them have noticed that Fatuulu never reappeared.

It is, however, an interesting fact that in 1952 – the year before Belle's death – a young Dane named Preben Kauffmann landed in Tonga, having six months earlier left San Francisco in a small, second-hand boat. Sailing boldly under Golden Gate Bridge and out into the Pacific, he reached the South Seas kingdom by way of Tahiti. After a short time he settled on Tafahi – not, curiously enough, near the village on the north coast, but in the south-east; in other words, on the beach where the fish-god had got up to his tricks 60 years before. Preben Kauffmann discovered a cave behind the beach, converted it into a comfortable home, and spent the next 40 years of his life there as a hermit.

PREBEN VIGO HEINRICH KAUFFMANN was born at Fredericia, not far from the Schleswig-Holstein border, on 11 June 1923 – on the back seat of the taxi that was rushing his mother to hospital. A sickly but studious boy who nearly always gained top marks at his primary and secondary schools in the small Danish seaport of Skaelskør, he was just short of 17 when the Germans invaded Denmark on 9 April 1940. The following year he went to Copenhagen Polytechnic to study engineering. Having specialized in underwater construction, he graduated with distinction in 1946 and in 1948 moved to San Francisco, where he obtained a job as a bridge and tunnel inspector. Interestingly, he at once began to save up enough money to buy a sailing boat. After two years the time came: Preben Kauffmann, who knew nothing about boat-handling or navigation on the high seas, bought some sailing and navigation manuals and a cheap, second-hand single-master 26 feet long. Thus equipped, he devoted all his spare time to teaching himself seamanship by cruising around San Francisco Bay – under the eyes, so to speak, of 94-year-old Belle Osbourne, who had a splendid view of the bay from her house high above the city. At last, one fine day in the summer of 1951, he loaded up his boat with plenty of supplies and sailed out into the Pacific under Golden Gate Bridge.

He got to Tonga on 18 March 1952, tanned and flaxen-bearded after his long voyage and his detour via Tahiti. Although unable to speak the local language and almost penniless, he very soon established himself in the island kingdom. Instead of becoming a beach-comber like so many thousands of traumatized ex-soldiers who fled to the South Seas after the Second World War, he obtained an audience at the royal palace the day after his arrival. The same day, he made Queen Salote a gift of his boat and decided to settle in Tonga for the rest of his life. This is surprising in itself. Other foreigners have all, without exception, commented on the extreme difficulty of obtaining an audience at the Tongan court; before gaining entry they had to negotiate for weeks with court officials, submit requests in writing and send emissaries to the palace.

Kauffmann later attributed his swift acceptance to the Tongan government's satisfaction at having an engineer in the country. Offered the post of royal architect in his first year, he was unwilling to give up his freedom, preferring to remain attached to the royal house as a freelance adviser without a formal position or fixed salary. Queen Salote adopted him as her son shortly afterwards.

One would like to believe that the royal family had need of competent advisers. The crown prince, who later became King Taufa'ahau Tupou IV, was always endeavouring to modernize his kingdom in a wide variety of ways. He reformed the Tongan alphabet by doing away with the letters B and D because he considered P and T quite sufficient on their own. He planned to construct a 1.9-mile landing strip with Soviet aid, so that the very biggest jets could touch down on his doorstep. He proposed to plant olive groves on the Italian model and to compete with the Japanese whaling industry. When none of these schemes bore fruit he drilled for oil on his island. It is unknown what form of consultations took place between the Danish expatriate and the quixotic crown prince, but there is nothing to indicate that Preben Kauffmann performed any great feats of engineering in Tonga. The only evidence of his architectural activities is a wooden church in the Danish style on the main island, Tongatapu. On the other hand, he became renowned as the solitary, self-supporting white settler who, with the blessing of the royal family, spent his life on the beach at Tafahi. The islanders soon christened him 'Tavi Maupiti', meaning 'Breath that came from the sea' or, alternatively, 'the Unsurpassed'.

His activities on Tafahi are a mystery. He built himself a wooden platform in a breadfruit tree in the immediate vicinity of 'Fatuulu's Rock', went around naked, lived on mangos, coconuts and roots, and forbore to cut his hair and beard for decades. If his own account is to be believed,[1] the only tools he possessed were a machete, a magnifying glass, a pocket knife and a teaspoon. He spent the nights and the hottest hours of the day on his platform in the breadfruit tree. When it rained he withdrew to a nearby cave, where he also kept his library.

Preben Kauffmann stuck it out at his hermitage for ten years. Then he returned to civilization to serve as Queen Salote's personal adviser on the main island of Tongatapu. Even then, however, he regularly returned to Tafahi with the queen's blessing and spent the hottest six months of the year on the beach near Fatuulu's Rock.

It should be pointed out that Tafahi makes a wholly unsuitable holiday resort during the six summer months. The climate is terribly hot and humid, more so than anywhere else in the Kingdom of Tonga. It rains several times a day and hurricanes are a constant threat. The steep slopes immediately behind the beach are clothed in impenetrable jungle, and there is nothing for a solitary visitor to do. Although it is true that tropical fruits literally fall into your lap – there are coconuts, mangos and pawpaws in abundance – it remains a mystery why a young Danish engineer should have chosen to spend his life on the beach in this of all places. Kauffmann's mother, who visited him once in later years, is supposed to have said that it wasn't even a good enough spot to die in.

When 'Tavi' was still a young man, he sometimes, in his solitude, entertained the idea of marriage. He confided his plan to Queen Salote, who pointed out that, in Tonga, a man married not only his bride but her entire clan as well, and that this could lead to unpleasantness. So he abandoned the idea. The only time he ever succumbed to temptation was during the dry season in 1969, when the Peace Corps sent a pretty 24-year-old American girl named Tina Martin to Tonga to teach English. Kauffmann fell in love with Tina, who had won the title 'Miss Columbia' at her high school in South Carolina a few years before.[2] He sometimes jokingly referred to her as his 'girlfriend',[3] but she told him that he was too like Jesus Christ in character and appearance and she too unlike Mary Magdalene. To that he meaningfully retorted that he wasn't as much of an ascetic as she thought. When her teaching assignment ended in October 1971, Tina returned to California. She was destined to be the only woman in Preben Kauffmann's life. They corresponded for many years, even when Tina had long been married and was the mother of a son, and did not lose contact until the 1980s.

When newspaper reporters asked Preben Kauffmann what his motives were for living like a hermit, the reasons he gave were diverse in the extreme. In 1987 he told the Tongan news magazine *Matangi*

Tonga that he had fled to the far side of the world as a young man to escape the atomic ravages of a Third World War. 'I realized it was maybe not enough to go to Australia. I had to get even further afield to a place where there was nothing worthwhile wasting an atomic bomb on.'[4] A less obvious reason can scarcely be imagined, given that the nuclear powers embarked on their atomic tests in the South Seas two years after Preben Kauffmann's arrival. In the Marshall Islands on 1 March 1954 the USA exploded its first experimental hydrogen bomb, which was a thousand times more powerful than the bombs dropped on Hiroshima and Nagasaki. Furthermore, Britain and France regularly used the Pacific for atomic tests in the ensuing four decades.

The explanation Kauffmann gave the Danish paper *Yillands Posten* in 1991 was scarcely more credible: that the Tongan climate was good for his rheumatism and tuberculosis. It was not, however, lost on the reporter that he could scarcely move for pain in the joints and shortness of breath.

So time went by. Kauffmann spent half the year on Tafahi near Fatuulu's Rock – which had long since been renamed 'Tavi's Rock' – and the rest of the time down south at the court of Salote, his queen and adoptive mother. It cannot be said that the Tongan climate was particularly beneficial to him. He suffered from rheumatism and heart trouble, and because he was a vegetarian whose diet consisted entirely of fruit and greenstuff, the effects of protein deficiency became noticeable over the years. When he was 68, Kauffmann had had enough. He wrote to the Danish ambassador in New Zealand requesting an air ticket home to Denmark.

At the end of January 1992, after almost 40 years in the Pacific, he bade Tonga a quiet and unobtrusive farewell without taking leave of the royal family or his many friends. Some 36 hours later, on 1 February 1992, he emerged from the plane at Copenhagen in bitterly cold weather wearing a threadbare shirt, a checked jacket, a Polynesian floral kilt, and a pair of down-at-heel old shoes on his bare feet. He had no articles of value to declare.

He took refuge at Skaelskør with his sister Elsbeth, who had never married and was still living in their late parents' home. Denmark's social security system gave its stray lamb a kindly welcome: Preben Kauffmann was awarded a monthly old age pension – probably more money than he had ever possessed in his life – and provided with medicines for his rheumatism and his weak heart. Despite this, he could not get used to living in the chilly north. He spent whole days in bed and often shed nostalgic tears for the warmth and the wide open expanses of the South Seas. He suffered from chronic colds and his rheumatism grew steadily worse. He knew no one apart from his sister. Three years after his homecoming, on 11 April 1995, he took an overdose of his cardiac pills. The medical examiner defined the cause of death as heart failure.

Epilogue

WELL, THAT'S ALL. A year has gone by since that evening outside the Outrigger Hotel, high above Apia. Having crossed the island on foot, I'm now convinced that Stevenson would have taken no more than three hours to reach the south coast on horseback. I called on his friends' grandchildren and talked with them at length, but none of them could give me any information about a small volcanic island just below the horizon. I spent whole afternoons at Vailima and discovered all kinds of interesting things; for instance that the wine cellar referred to by innumerable biographers – the one from which Stevenson is said to have fetched a bottle of burgundy on the last day of his life – simply doesn't exist. The house stands on stilts and never had a cellar, nor is there anything resembling a cellar above ground either. Although interesting, this is hardly in the same league as pirate treasure and treasure-hunters. I found no Spanish gold doubloons at Vailima, but there is a massive safe in the drawing-room at the exact spot where one used to stand in Stevenson's day. Needless to say, not only is it empty but – despite the museum guide's assurances – it bears not the slightest resemblance to the safe that can be seen in Stevenson's family photographs.

I also found the river basin in which Stevenson used to bathe and took a dip in it myself. I climbed the steep path up Mount Vaea and spent an hour beside Stevenson's grave – without, alas, experiencing any metaphysical sensations. While Nadja and the children were spending days and weeks looking for nemo fish on Vavau Beach, I combed every library in Samoa, pestered five missionaries and three university professors, and ambushed two government ministers.

I also investigated rumours which no one would corroborate. One of them was that the King of Tonga had recovered a 19th-century hoard of gold from the wreck of a ship off the Ha'apai Islands and sold it to the Japanese billionaire Ryoichi Sasakawa for $300 million in the early 1990s – in other words, just when Preben Kauffmann quit the South Seas and went home to die in his chilly native land, penniless and miserable (and cheated out of his finder's reward?). Unfortunately, Sasakawa had died in the interim and the Tongan royal house regretted to inform me that it had no knowledge of any hoard of gold or any $300 million.

FIVE WEEKS were long enough. The children had to go back to school. We said goodbye and flew home.

What still annoys me is the fact that I never managed to set foot on my real objective, the beach in the south of Tafahi. I had wanted to touch Fatuulu's Rock, locate the cave in which Preben Kauffmann spent much of his life, and picture Captain Thompson's crew rowing the treasure chests ashore. That done, perhaps I would have looked around – why not? – a little further inland. Unfortunately, Royal Tongan Airlines – the only airline that offered occasional flights to Tafahi in a little twin-engined prop plane – went bankrupt shortly before my arrival in the South Seas. There was a ferry, but it sailed only once every six weeks, and not from Samoa. Even if I'd abandoned my family and flown at once to Tongatapu by Air New Zealand, I'd have missed the boat by 36 hours.

A year has gone by since then. Our children have grown. The eldest now has a girlfriend, the youngest is out of nappies. We had really meant to stay at home this summer.

But now we're back here again. The children are happy to be reunited with their nemo fish, Nadja is happy the children are happy, and I would be happy if Royal Tongan Airlines resurrected itself, or if a ferry appeared on the horizon.

Vavu Beach, Samoa, *18 July 2005*

'I like biography far better than fiction myself; fiction is too free. In biography you have your little handful of facts, like bits of a puzzle, and you sit down and fit 'em together this way and that, and get up and throw 'em down, and say damn, and go out for a walk. And it's real soothing; and when done, gives an idea of finish to the writer that is very peaceful. Of course, it's not really so finished as quite a rotten novel; it always has and always must have the incurable illogicalities of life about it, the fathoms of slack and the miles of circuitous tedium. Still, that's where the fun comes in.'[1]

Robert Louis Stevenson to Sir Edmund Gosse

18 June 1893

Notes and Sources

Extracts from the letters of Robert Louis Stevenson are taken from the following throughout:

Letters: Colvin, Sidney (ed), *The Letters of Robert Louis Stevenson to his Family and Friends*, 2 Vols (New York: 1902).

Miscellanies: Colvin, Sidney (ed), *Letters And Miscellanies of Robert Louis Stevenson: Correspondence Addressed to Sidney Colvin, November 1890 to October 1894* (New York: 1909)

Epigraph

1. Robert Louis Stevenson, *The Ebb-Tide* in *The Works of Robert Louis Stevenson* (Vailima, London: 1922), Vol 18, p 124. Hereafter *Works*.

Chapter 1

1. *Letters* Vol II, p 197.
2. *Letters*, Vol II, p 200.
3. William E Clarke, 'Robert Louis Stevenson in Samoa', *Yale Review* (January 1921) p 275.
4. Harry Jay Moors, *With Stevenson in Samoa* (London: 1911) p 2.
5. *Letters,* Vol II, p 207.
6. Otto Riedel, *Der Kampf um Deutsch-Samoa* (Berlin: 1938) p 218.
7. *Letters,* Vol II, p 208.
8. William E Clarke's handwritten annual reports are held in the archives of the London Missionary Society. Louis's handwritten notes are preserved in the Beinecke Rare Book and Manuscript Library, Yale University. Some have been published in Graham

Balfour, *The Life of Robert Louis Stevenson* (New York: 1901), Vol 2, p 102.

Chapter 2

1. Stevenson went on to tell the doctor how he proposed to cure his diseased respiratory tracts: 'Now you would have gone longer yet without news of your truant patient, but that I have a medical discovery to communicate. I find I can (almost immediately) fight off a cold with liquid extract of coca; two or (if obstinate) three teaspoonfuls in the day for a variable period of from one to five days sees the cold generally to the door. I find it at once produces a glow, stops rigour, and though it makes one very uncomfortable, prevents the advance of the disease. Hearing of this influenza, it occurred to me that this might prove remedial; and perhaps a stronger exhibition – injections of cocaine, for instance – still better.' *Letters,* Vol II, p 209.
2. *Miscellanies,* p 32.
3. *Letters,* Vol II, p 212.
4. Information from Naumati Vasa, teacher of traditional carving and mythology at the National University of Samoa, Apia.
5. *Letters.*
6. Fanny and Robert Louis Stevenson (ed Charles Neider), *Our Samoan Adventure* (New York: 1956) p 38.
7. Fanny and Robert Louis Stevenson, *Our Samoan Adventure,* p 91.
8. Quoted in Margaret Mackay, *The Violent Friend* (London: 1969).
9. Moors, *With Stevenson in Samoa* p 210.
10. Lloyd Osbourne, *An Intimate Portrait of Robert Louis Stevenson* (New York: 1924) p 134.
11. Louis casually mentions Mount Vaea in a letter to Sidney Colvin in December 1891, in which he describes his search for a source of drinking water. See *Letters,* Vol 7, p 22.
12. *Sydney Morning Herald,* 14 February 1890.

Chapter 3

1. Robert Louis Stevenson, 'My first book: Treasure Island', in *Works,* Vol 5.
2. Letters from Fanny Stevenson to her Californian admirer Timothy Rearden, 25 July and 13 December 1876, now in the possession of the Silverado Museum, St Helena, California, quoted in Mackay, *The Violent Friend*, p. 42 ff.
3. Mackay, *The Violent Friend*, p 41.
4. Mackay, *The Violent Friend*, pp 49–50.
5. Robert Louis Stevenson, *Travels with a Donkey in the Cévennes*, in *Works,* Vol 1, p 209.
6. Stevenson, *Travels with a Donkey,* in *Works,* Vol 1, p 297.
7. Unpublished letter to Sidney Colvin, Beinicke Collection, Yale University.
8. Robert Louis Stevenson, *The Amateur Emigrant* in *Works,* Vol 2, p 234 ff.
9. Letter to Sidney Colvin, 20 August 1879, in *Letters,* Vol I, p 170.
10. Letter to Henley, August 1879, in *Letters,* Vol 3, p 10.
11. George Bancroft, *History of the United States* (Boston: 1841). Louis bought the six volumes on 19 August 1879, while waiting for the train to California.
12. Osbourne, *An Intimate Portrait,* p 21.
13. Letter to Charles Baxter, 9 September 1879, in *Letters*.
14. Letter to Sidney Colvin, September 1879 in *Letters,* Vol I, p 171.
15. Robert Louis Stevenson, 'The Old and the New Pacific Capital', in *Works,* Vol 2, p 410.
16. Stevenson, 'The Old and the New Pacific Capital', in *Works,* Vol 2, p 433.
17. *The San Francisco Call,* 31 October 1879, p 1. An almost identical article appeared in the *Santa Barbara Daily Press,* 28 October 1879, p 2.

Chapter 4

1. Captain James Colnett, *A Voyage into the South Atlantic and Round Cape Hoorn into the Pacific Ocean* (London: 1798; facsimile edition Amsterdam and New York: 1968) p 78..
2. *New York Times,* 1 December 1897 and 13 March 1898.

Chapter 5

1. *Letters.*
2. *Letters.*
3. *Letters.*
4. Quoted in Mackay, *The Violent Friend*, p 119.
5. *Letters*, Vol I, p 236.
6. Robert Louis Stevenson, *Treasure Island*, in *Works*, Vol 5, p 62.
7. Stevenson, *Treasure Island*, in *Works*, Vol 5, p 22.
8. Stevenson, *Treasure Island*, in *Works*, Vol 5, p 24.
9. Stevenson, *Treasure Island*, in *Works*, Vol 5, p 27
10. For sources relating to variations on the name Walter, e.g. Woggle, Woggs, Woggy, Watty, Wiggs, also Bogue, see Willem George Lockett, *Robert Louis Stevenson at Davos* (London: nd), p 58; Joseph C Furnas, *A Voyage to Windward: The Life of Robert Louis Stevenson* (New York: 1951), p 189; Ralph Hancock and Julian Weston, *The Lost Treasure of Cocos Island* (New York: 1960), p 39 ff.

Chapter 6

1. Letter from August Gissler to his brother Hermann, December 1888; now held by Gissler's estate, part of which is administered by Hermann Gissler's grandson, Dr Richard Gissler of Jülich.
2. *New York Times*, 20 November 1904.

Chapter 7

1. Louis had already written a first version of *The Bottle Imp* in Hawaii in May 1889, and he wrote another immediately after his arrival in Samoa at the end of that year. He derived his inspiration from a stage play of the same name by Richard Brinsley Peake, premiered at the English Opera House in 1828. That play, in turn, was based on a short story by Hans Jacob Christoph von Grimmelshausen (1622–76): *Trutz Simplex. Die Lebensbeschreibung der Erzbetrügerin und Landstörzerin Courasche* (1669), Chapters 18–22.
2. Robert Louis Stevenson, *The Bottle Imp*, in *Works*, Vol 15, p 402.
3. Stevenson, *The Bottle Imp*, in *Works*, Vol 15, p 395.
4. *Letters*, Vol II, pp 59–60.

Chapter 8

1. See John Martin, *An Account of the Natives of the Tonga Islands in the South Pacific Ocean* (London: 1817), Vol 2, p 91. In the ensuing decades, more and more adventurers sought underwater access to the cave in which the treasure of the *Port au Prince* was reputed to be. Most of them did so without the requisite police authorization, as King Taufa'ahau recalled in his biography, and regardless of the fact that the gold was legally the property of the Kingdom of Tonga.

Chapter 9

1. Jacob Le Maire, *Mirror of the Australian Navigation: The Voyage of Jacob Le Maire and William Schouten, 1615–1616* (Amsterdam: 1754; facsimile edition, Sydney: 1999),

Chapter 10

1. Balfour, *Life*, Vol 2, p 123.
2. All these quotations from *Letters*, Vol II, p 444 *et al* and from *Miscellanies*.
3. From an interview in the *Christchurch Press*, 24 April 1893.
4. Osbourne, *An Intimate Portrait*, p 130.
5. Fanny and Robert Louis Stevenson, *Our Samoan Adventure*, p 243.
6. Before releasing Stevenson's original letters to the printer, Colvin stuck two strips of paper, one black and one white, over any passages that afforded an intimate glimpse of the author's family life. In 1913 he sold these censored letters to the Widener Collection at Harvard. Its administrators imposed a decades-long ban on removing the strips of paper for fear of defacing the handwriting beneath. They did not revoke it until 1962, when the strips were removed without difficulty and the passages cited above came to light. See Bradford A Booth, 'The Vailima Letters of Robert Louis Stevenson', *Harvard Library Bulletin*, Vol XV, No 2, (April 1967), pp 117–28.)
7. Booth, 'The Vailima Letters of Robert Louis Stevenson', *Harvard Library Bulletin*, Vol XV, No 2, (April 1967), p 125.
8. Booth, 'The Vailima Letters of Robert Louis Stevenson', *Harvard Library Bulletin*, Vol XV, No 2, (April 1967), p 124.

9. *Miscellanies,* p 167.

10. *Miscellanies,* p 214.

11. *Letters.*

12. *Miscellanies,* p 218.

13. 5 April was a Wednesday, not a Thursday. Robert Louis Stevenson often lost track of dates and days of the week in his isolated island home.

14. *Miscellanies,* pp 222–3.

Chapter 11

1. The strange happenings on Tafahi. The American ethnologist Edward Winslow Gifford was told all these things by Chief Maatu. Precise dating is impossible because the inhabitants of Tafahi had no form of chronometry at the time. Maatu did, however, recall that the incidents he described occurred during the reign of Ngongo, or at the end of the 19th century. See Edward Winslow Gifford, *Tongan Society* (Honolulu: 1929), p 314.

Chapter 12

1. Fanny Stevenson, *The Cruise of the 'Janet Nichol': A Diary by Mrs Robert Louis Stevenson* (London: 1915), p 4.

Chapter 13

1. Balfour, *Life*, Vol 2, p 178.

2. This fragment was preserved for posterity by Arthur Johnstone in *Recollections of Robert Louis Stevenson in the Pacific* (London: 1905), p 309.

Chapter 14

1. On Isabel Strong on Stevenson's death, see Isobel Osbourne Field, *This Life I've Loved* (New York and Toronto: 1937). On Stevenson's death, see *Letters,* Vol 8, p 401 ff; from Belle Strong's diary. On Stevenson's burial, see also Nelson Eustis, 'R. L. Stevenson's Days in Samoa', in *Aggie Grey of Samoa* (Adelaide: 1970), pp 30–3.

Chapter 15

1. Details from letter from Charles Baxter to Graham Balfour, 3
   November 1897; letter from Stevenson to Charles Baxter, *c.* 17
   June 1893, in DeLancey Ferguson and Marshall Waingrow (ed),
   RLS: Stevenson's letters to Charles Baxter (New Haven: 1956)
   p 337.
2. See *New York Times,* 22 September 1936.
3. See *New York Times,* 23 May 1947. On Osbourne's admiration
   for Mussolini, see Lloyd Osbourne, *20 Letters to Isobel Field,
   July–December 1940,* unpublished correspondence in the
   Bancroft Library, University of California, Berkeley, California.

Chapter 16

1. Interview in *Matangi Tonga,* September/October 1987.
2. The beauty queen election should have taken place on 22
   November 1963 but had to be postponed for a fortnight
   because that was the day on which President John F Kennedy
   was assassinated in Dallas. Tina Martin later wrote a short
   story about a girl from the southern states who prays to God
   to fix the election in her favour on the day of Kennedy's
   murder. This can be read at http://www.peacecorpswriters.org/
   pages/2003/0305/305wrwr-tm.html.
3. Correspondence between Tina Martin and the author,
   September–October 2004.
4. Interview in *Matangi Tonga,* September/October 1987.

Epigraph

1. *Letters,* Vol II, pp 390–1.

Bibliography

Baarslag, Karl, *Islands of Adventure* (New York: 1940).

Balfour, Graham, *The Life of Robert Louis Stevenson,* 2 Vols (New York: 1901).

Banfield, M A, *The Health Biographies of Alexander Leeper, Robert Louis Stevenson and Fanny Stevenson* (Moodbury, South Australia: 2001).

Bathurst, Bella, *The Lighthouse Stevensons* (London: 1999).

Beer, Karl-Theo, *Samoa – eine Reise in den Tod. Briefe des Obermatrosen Adolph Thamm, S. M. Kanonenboot Eber 1887–1889* (Hamburg: 1994).

Bell, Ian, *Dreams of Exile: Robert Louis Stevenson: A Biography* (New York: 1992).

Bermann, Richard A, *Home from the Sea: Robert Louis Stevenson in Samoa* (Indianapolis/New York: 1939).

Bohn, Robert, *Die Piraten* (Munich: 2003).

Booth, Bradford A, 'The Vailima Letters of Robert Louis Stevenson', *Harvard Library Bulletin* (April 1967).

Cairney, John, *The Quest for Robert Louis Stevenson* (Edinburgh: 2004).

Calder, Jenni, *RLS: A Life Study* (Glasgow: 1980).

Calder, Jenni, *The Robert Louis Stevenson Companion* (Edinburgh: 1980).

Caldwell, Elsie Noble, *Last Witness for Robert Louis Stevenson* (Norman: 1960).

Clarke, William E, 'Robert Louis Stevenson in Samoa', *Yale Review* (January 1921).

Cleator, Philip Ellaby, *Treasure for the Taking* (London: 1960).

Colley, Ann C, *Robert Louis Stevenson and the Colonial Imagination* (Hampshire/Burlington: 2004).

Colnett, James, *A Voyage into the South Atlantic and Round Cape Horn into the Pacific Ocean* (London: 1798; facsimile edition Amsterdam and New York: 1968).

Colvin, Sidney (ed), *The Letters of Robert Louis Stevenson to his Family and Friends*, 2 Vols (New York: 1902).

Colvin, Sidney (ed), *Letters And Miscellanies of Robert Louis Stevenson: Correspondence Addressed to Sidney Colvin, November 1890 to October 1894* (New York: 1909)

Colvin, Sidney, *Memories and Notes* (London: 1921).

Disch-Lauxmann, Peter, *Die authentische Geschichte von Stevensons 'Schatzinsel'* (Hamburg: 1985).

Eustis, Nelson, 'R. L. Stevenson's Days in Samoa', *Aggie Grey of Samoa* (Adelaide: 1970).

Eustis, Nelson, *The King of Tonga: A Biography* (Adelaide: 1997).

Field Osbourne Strong, Isobel, *This Life I've Loved* (New York: 1937).

Field Osbourne Strong, Isobel, 'Vailima Table-Talk: Robert Louis Stevenson in his "Home Life"', *Scribner's Magazine* (New York: June 1896).

Fitzpatrick, Elayne Wareing, *A Quixotic Companionship: Fanny and Robert Louis Stevenson* (Monterey: 1997).

Fletcher, Brunsdon, *Stevenson's Germany: The Case Against Germany in the Pacific* (London: 1920).

Fraser, Marie, *In Stevenson's Samoa* (London: 1895).

Furnas, Joseph C, *Voyage to Windward: The Life of Robert Louis Stevenson* (New York: 1951).

Gifford, Edward Winslow, *Tongan Myths and Tales* (Honolulu: 1924).

Gifford, Edward Winslow, *Tongan Society* (Honolulu: 1929).

Gilson, Richard Phillip, *Samoa 1830–1900: The Politics of a Multi-cultural Community* (Melbourne: 1970).

Grift Sanchez, Nellie van de, *The Life of Robert Louis Stevenson* (New York: 1920).

Hancock, Ralph and Weston, Julian, *The Lost Treasure of Cocos Island* (New York: 1960).

Harman, Claire, *Robert Louis Stevenson: A Biography* (London: 2004).

Hellman, George S, *The True Stevenson: A Study in Clarification* (Boston: 1925).

Hellman, George S, 'R.L.S. and the Streetwalker', *The American Mercury* (July 1936).

Issler, Anne Roller, *Happier for His Presence: San Francisco and Robert Louis Stevenson* (Stanford, California:1940).

Heyerdahl, Thor, *Kon-Tiki: Across the Pacific in a Raft* (London: 1948).

Johnstone, Arthur, *Recollections of Robert Louis Stevenson in the Pacific* (London: 1905).

Knight, Alanna, *Robert Louis Stevenson Treasury* (London: 1985).

Le Maire, Jacob, *Mirror of the Australian Navigation: The Voyage of Jacob Le Maire and William Schouten, 1615–1616* (Amsterdam: 1754; facsimile edition Sydney: 1999).

Lockett, William George, *Robert Louis Stevenson at Davos* (London: 1934).

Mackay, Margaret, *The Violent Friend: The Story of Mrs Robert Louis Stevenson* (New York: 1969).

Martin, John, *An Account of the Natives of the Tonga Island in the South Pacific Ocean. With an Original Grammar and Vocabulary of their Language. Compiled and Arranged from the Extensive Communications of Mr William Mariner, Several Years Resident in Those Islands,* 2 Vols (London: 1817).

McLynn, Frank, *Robert Louis Stevenson* (London: 1993).

Moors, Harry Jay, *With Stevenson in Samoa* (London: 1911).

Moors, Harry Jay, *Some Recollections of Early Samoa* (Apia: 1986).

Osbourne, Katherine Durham, *Robert Louis Stevenson in California* (Chicago: 1911).

Osbourne, Lloyd, *An Intimate Portrait of Robert Louis Stevenson* (New York: 1924).

Osbourne, Lloyd, 'Mr Stevenson's Home Life at Vailima', *Scribner's Magazine* (New York: October 1895).

Osbourne, Lloyd, '20 Letters to Isobel Field, July–December 1940', unpublished (Bancroft Library, University of California, Berkeley, California).

Pekalkiewicz, Janusz, *Da liegt Gold: Verborgene Schätze in aller Welt* (Stuttgart: 1997).

Platt, Cameron and Wright, John, *Treasure Islands: The Fascinating World of Pirates, Buried Treasures and Fortune Hunters* (London: 1992).

Riedel, Otto, *Der Kampf um Deutsch-Samoa: Erinnerungen eines Hamburger Kaufmanns* (Berlin: 1938).

Rutherford, Noel, *Friendly Islands: A History of Tonga* (Melbourne: 1977).

Saint-Martin, Vivien de, *Nouveau Dictionnaire de Géographie Universelle* (Paris: 1879).

Sibree, James, *Register of L.M.S. Missionaries* (London: 1923).

Solf, Wilhelm Heinrich (ed), *The Cyclopedia of Samoa (Illustrated)* (Sydney: 1907).

Steuart, John Alexander, *Robert Louis Stevenson: A Critical Biography* (Boston: 1924).

Stevenson, Fanny, *The Cruise of the 'Janet Nichol': A Diary by Mrs Robert Louis Stevenson* (London: 1915).

Stevenson, Fanny and Robert Louis (Neider, Charles (ed)), *Our Samoan Adventure* (New York: 1956).

Stevenson, Robert Louis, *The Works of Robert Louis Stevenson,* 26 Vols (Vailima Edition, London: 1922).

Stevenson, Robert Louis (ed Booth, Bradford A. and Mehew, Ernest), *The Letters of Robert Louis Stevenson,* 8 Vols (New Haven and London: 1994–5).

Stevenson, Robert Louis, *Letters and Miscellanies: Correspondence Addressed to Sidney Colvin, November 1890 to October 1894* (New York: 1904).

Stevenson, Robert Louis, *Letters to Charles Baxter* (New Haven: 1956).

Swearingen, Roger G, *The Prose Writings of Robert Louis Stevenson: A Guide* (Hamden, Connecticut: 1980).

Terry, Reginald Charles, *Robert Louis Stevenson: Interviews and Recollections* (Iowa: 1996).

Theroux, Joseph, 'Rediscovering "H.J.M", Samoa's "Unconquerable" Harry Moors', *Pacific Island Monthly* (August and September 1981).

Weiner, Michael A, *Secrets of Fijian Medicine* (Berkeley, *c* 1980).

Watson, Robert Mackenzie, *History of Samoa* (Auckland: 1918).

Whitmee, S J, 'Tusitala. R.L.S – A New Phase', *The Atlantic Monthly* (March 1923).

Wilson, Derek, *The World Atlas of Treasure* (London: 1981).

Woodhead, Richard, *The Strange Case of R.L. Stevenson* (Edinburgh: 2001).

Acknowledgements

THIS BOOK would never have been written but for my friend Walter Hurni of Blenheim, New Zealand. It was he who, many years ago, made the exciting discovery that a second Cocos Island exists not far from Robert Louis Stevenson's Samoa. In the course of our long conversations, he was generous enough to share with me the results of his years of research in the South Seas, and he was always available when I got stuck.

I also owe a debt of gratitude to Dr Richard Gissler of Jülich, who gave me access to his uncle August's letters; likewise to Patrick Moors of Apia, grandson of Stevenson's friend Harry Moors; to Trevor Stevenson of Apia, the author's lawyer great-grandnephew, for his hospitality and his assistance on Samoa's diplomatic dance floor; to Tina Martin of San Francisco for information about her onetime friend Preben Kauffmann; and to the many university and library experts who allowed me to share in their specialized knowledge: Unasa Leulu Felise Va'a, professor of history, and Naumati Vasa, lecturer on wood carving and mythology at the National University of Samoa, Apia; Dean Solofa, Climate Scientific Officer at the Samoan Ministry of Agriculture; the Reverend Oka Fau'olo, Chairman of the Samoa Council of Churches; Roger G Swearingen, leading Stevenson expert of Santa Rosa, California; Professor Richard Dury, Bergamo University, Italy, whose website (http://dinamico.unibg.it/rls/rls.htm) is the most important source of information for Stevensonians the world over; Yaye Tang and Lisa Cole, School of Oriental and African Studies, University of London; Liza Verity, National Maritime Museum, Greenwich; Kathy Wilkinson, Council for World Mission, London; Elaine Greig, curator of The Writers' Museum, Edinburgh; Chris Quist, curator of the Stevenson Museum at Monterey, California; Don Clarke, Chairman of the Los

Angeles Basin Geological Society and geologist at the Department of Oil Properties in the city administration of Long Beach; William P Stoneman and Florence Fearrington, *Harvard Library Bulletin*; Leif Møller, journalist and Preben Kauffmann biographer of Ry, Denmark; Slobodan Bob Milinovic, State Library of New South Wales, Sydney, Australia; Nina Rothberg for research at San Francisco Public Library, California; Namrata Krishna for research at the UC Berkeley Library, California; and, last but not least, Canton Solothurn, Switzerland, who produced my airline tickets to London, Edinburgh, Los Angeles and Samoa.